THE REMINISCENCES OF Admiral Frederick H. Michaelis U.S. Navy (Retired)

INTERVIEWED BY
Dr. John T. Mason, Jr.

U.S. Naval Institute • Annapolis, Maryland

Copyright © 1996

Preface

For more than two decades--first for Columbia University, later for the Naval Institute--Dr. John T. Mason, Jr., conducted oral history interviews with retired naval officers. He wound up his career with this one, the memoir of Frederick H. Michaelis, the only member of the Naval Academy's class of 1940 who attained the rank of four-star admiral. The concluding interview with Admiral Michaelis was only a few weeks before Dr. Mason's retirement from the Naval Institute in June 1982.

This oral history tells of a career marked from the beginning by its involvement with the latest in technology. Even as an ensign in his first ship in 1941, Michaelis was responsible for the installation and operation of a new device known as radar. After undergoing flight training, he flew the new F6F Hellcat in combat strikes against the home islands of Japan. In the postwar years he remained at the forefront while serving in Air Development Squadron Three, then placing in commission the Naval Air Special Weapons Facility in New Mexico. He was subsequently one of the first two naval aviators to go through training as prospective commanding officers of the nuclear-powered aircraft carrier Enterprise. As a flag officer, he commanded a carrier task group in combat in the Vietnam War, helped devise the nation's planning for the targeting of nuclear weapons, commanded Naval Air Force Atlantic Fleet, and was in charge of the Navy's entire procurement program as Chief of Naval Material.

In the course of moving from the initial raw transcript of the oral interviews to this final version, I have done some slight editing in the interests of accuracy, smoothness, and clarity. I have added footnotes to provide further information for those using the volume. Admiral Michaelis's widow and son have given their blessing to this completed version. Ms. Ann Hassinger of the Naval Institute's history division has made a significant contribution through her diligence in the overall process of printing, proofreading, and overseeing the binding of the completed volume.

                                                        Paul Stillwell
                                                        Director, History Division
                                                       U.S. Naval Institute
                                                       August 1996

ADMIRAL FREDERICK HAYES MICHAELIS
UNITED STATES NAVY (RETIRED)

Frederick Hayes Michaelis was born in Kansas City, Missouri, on 4 March 1917, son of Frederick Henry and Mabel A. (Hayes) Michaelis. He attended Kansas City Junior College for two years, prior to entering the U.S. Naval Academy, Annapolis, Maryland, on appointment from his native state in 1936. Graduated and commissioned ensign on 6 June 1940, he was subsequently promoted with the following dates of rank: lieutenant (junior grade), 15 April 1942; lieutenant, 1 October 1942; lieutenant commander, 17 October 1944; commander, 1 January 1951; captain, 1 April 1959; rear admiral, 1 December 1965; vice admiral, 1 September 1969; admiral, 18 April 1975.

Following graduation from the Naval Academy in 1940, Ensign Michaelis reported aboard the USS Pennsylvania (BB-38) and was on board that battleship, in dry dock at Pearl Harbor, Territory of Hawaii, when the Japanese attacked there on 7 December 1941. Damaged during the attack, the Pennsylvania steamed, later that month, for San Francisco, California. After undergoing repairs, she returned to Pearl Harbor in August 1942. Detached from that ship in October 1942, Michaelis received flight training at the naval air stations at New Orleans, Louisiana; Pensacola and Melbourne, Florida. Designated a naval aviator in June 1943, he was next a flight instructor at the Naval Air Station, Melbourne.

In March 1944 Michaelis joined Fighting Squadron 12 as flight officer, served as executive officer from May 1944 until February 1945, then assumed command. He was awarded the Navy Cross for leading a combat air patrol in the vicinity of Okinawa Jima on 17 April 1945, during which he shot down three hostile aircraft. He also received the Silver Star Medal for participating in the first carrier-based air attacks, operating from the USS Randolph (CV-15), on the Tokyo area on 16, 17, and 25 February 1945; during which he destroyed an enemy fighter plane. He was also awarded gold stars in lieu of the second, third, and fourth Air Medals and the Distinguished Flying Cross for completing 20 combat missions in the vicinity of the Japanese Empire and adjacent island chains during the period 16 February to 20 May 1945.

Detached from command of Fighting Squadron 12 in July 1945, Michaelis commanded Bombing Fighting Squadron Five until June 1946. Ordered to the Postgraduate School, Annapolis, Maryland, he received instruction in aeronautical engineering and in August 1949 completed the course at the Massachusetts Institute of Technology, Cambridge, from which he received the degree of master of science. He next served with Air Development Squadron Three, ten months as project coordinator and ten months as executive officer. In June 1951 he placed in commission and assumed command of the Naval Air Special Weapons Facility at Kirtland Air Force Base, Albuquerque, New Mexico. In February 1954 he became Commander Air Group 11, based on board the USS

Kearsarge (CVA-33). Detached from that command in June 1955, he reported the next month as special weapons officer on the staff of Commander Air Force Pacific Fleet.

From January 1956 to May 1957 he was special assistant to the Assistant Secretary of the Navy for Air, Navy Department, Washington, D.C., after which he served in the USS Randolph (CVA-15) as executive officer. Detached from that attack carrier in July 1958, he had instruction at the Naval War College, Newport, Rhode Island, and in February 1959 assumed command of the fleet oiler USS Tolovana (AO-64). Captain Michaelis had prospective commanding officer instruction in the Reactor Development Division, Bureau of Ships, Navy Department, during the period from December 1959 to December 1960, then was assigned to the Navy Plans Section, Division of Strategic Plans, Office of the Chief of Naval Operations, Navy Department.

In July 1963 Captain Michaelis took command of the USS Enterprise (CVAN-65) and in August 1965 became Director of Development Programs, Office of the Chief of Naval Operations. In September 1967, he reported as Commander Carrier Division Nine and as such also served as Commander Task Group 77.8 and as Yankee Station Commander. He was awarded the Legion of Merit for ". . . outstanding leadership, professional skill, and sound judgment in the direction of combat operations against significant military targets and lines of communication in North Vietnam . . . " He was also entitled to wear the ribbon for and a facsimile of the Navy Unit Commendation awarded to the USS Oriskany (CVA-34), which was flagship of Commander Carrier Division Nine.

From August 1968 to September 1969 he was Assistant Chief of Naval Operations (Air), Navy Department. In September 1969 he was promoted to vice admiral and served from then to February 1972 as Deputy Director of the Joint Strategic Target Planning Staff, Offutt Air Force Base, Nebraska. From February 1972 to February 1975 he served as Commander Naval Air Force, U.S. Atlantic Fleet, with additional duty as Commander Fleet Air, Norfolk, Virginia. He was promoted to four-star admiral and served as Chief of Naval Material from April 1975 until his retirement from active duty on 1 August 1978.

Following retirement he worked with various organizations, including the Association of Naval Aviation, Naval Aviation Museum, Tailhook Association, The Retired Officers Association, Naval Academy Foundation, and the Vinson Hall Foundation. He also served on corporate boards in the public and private sectors. In 1992 he was inducted into the Carrier Aviation Hall of Fame on board the carrier Yorktown at Charleston, South Carolina. Admiral Michaelis died at the Walter Reed Army Medical Center in Washington, D.C., on 13 August 1992.

In addition to the Navy Cross; the Silver Star Medal; the Legion of Merit; the Distinguished Flying Cross; the Air Medal with three gold stars; and the Navy Unit Commendation ribbon, Admiral Michaelis received the American Defense Service Medal with star; American Campaign Medal; Asiatic-Pacific Campaign Medal with silver star (five engagements); World War II Victory Medal; Navy Occupation Service Medal, Asia Clasp; National Defense Service Medal with bronze star; and the Vietnam Service Medal with two stars. He was also awarded the Republic of Vietnam National Order Fourth Class with rosette; the Republic of Vietnam Cross of Gallantry Army Level with bronze palm; and the Republic of Vietnam Campaign Medal.

Admiral Michaelis was married to the former Rose Schiche of Lake Geneva, Wisconsin. Their three children are Frederick Hayes Michaelis, Jr.; Molly Anne Fine; and Polly Michel Copansky.

Authorization

The U.S. Naval Institute is hereby authorized to make available to individuals, libraries, and other repositories of its choosing the transcripts of five oral history interviews concerning the life and career of the late Admiral Frederick H. Michaelis. The interviews were recorded on 9 November 1981, 19 November 1981, 29 January 1982, 8 March 1982, and 21 April 1982 in collaboration with Dr. John T. Mason for the U.S. Naval Institute.

The undersigned does hereby release and assign to the U.S. Naval Institute all right, title, restrictions, and interest in the interviews. The copyright in both the oral and transcribed versions shall be the sole property of the U.S. Naval Institute. The tape recordings of the interviews are and will remain the property of the U.S. Naval Institute.

Signed and sealed this _15TH_ day of _JULY_ 1996.

Rose S. Michaelis
Mrs. Frederick H. Michaelis, for the estate of
Admiral Frederick H. Michaelis, USN (Ret.)

Interview Number 1 with Admiral Frederick H. Michaelis, U.S. Navy (Retired)

Place: Naval Historical Center, Washington, D.C.

Date: Monday, 9 November 1981

Interviewer: John T. Mason, Jr.

Q: Admiral, I am delighted you have finally consented to do this series of interviews, because your career is a notable one in the Navy. What you have to say about your career should be of great value to historians of the present and of the future. As you understand, this is in the nature of a talking biography, so would you begin by giving me the date of your birth, the place of your birth, and something about your immediate family.

Admiral Michaelis: All right. I was born in Kansas City, Missouri, on March 4, 1917. I had one sister who was two and one-half years older than myself, and that constituted the children of the family. My father was an architect--in actuality, an architectural engineer--for the great span of his working life.

Q: Practicing in Kansas City?

Admiral Michaelis: He practiced in Kansas City, and he practiced in many states around. At one point in his life he had a most interesting and unusual occupation. He had built a couple of fraternity houses in the Middle West--a move to satisfy his fraternity brothers and reduce expenses for their building program. They were quite a success. The Midwest depended so much on fraternity and sorority houses to house their students.

Q: Especially at the state universities.

Admiral Michaelis: Yes, and they built big houses. He set up a company where he did all the designing and architectural work and helped them get the funding and so forth. His houses are still on the campuses of the universities of Kansas, Oklahoma, Missouri, Nebraska, and all those flat lands.

Q: What was the fraternity that triggered all of this?

Admiral Michaelis: He was a Sigma Chi, and that is where it all started.

Q: That was one of the most prominent fraternities.

Admiral Michaelis: My parents were both born and reared in Kansas City, Missouri. My grandfather was German and had come over from Germany between the First World War and the Second World War. My mother was originally a New Englander before my grandfather had married my grandmother and carried her to the great unknown of the Midwest--West Point landing on the Missouri River.

Q: They were indeed pioneers.

Admiral Michaelis: Yes, they were, and really both sides of the family were there in an agricultural and beef-raising community during the developmental period of the Midwest.

My dad studied with Frank Lloyd Wright but was never a strong advocate of his manner.*

Q: Was this in Chicago?

---

* Wright (1869-1959) was one of the best-known and most innovative American architects of the 20th century.

Admiral Michaelis: Yes. I should say that Dad worked with him rather than that he studied under him. The University of Pennsylvania and George Washington University here in Washington are where he had his education.

My early days were high school in Kansas City, and then I attended the Kansas City Junior College for two years before I went to the Naval Academy.

Q: Did you have any plans for your career other than the Navy at that point?

Admiral Michaelis: I had been strongly interested in flying, and I early became very much afflicted with the idea of flying off carriers. At one time I had decided to go into the cadet program of that time, 1934-1935; however, I was able to get appointed to the Naval Academy.[*] My parents were very strongly convinced that rather than stopping after a couple of years of college, I should finish college and go through the Navy regimen in that fashion, which I did.

Q: They were not opposed to a naval career, then?

Admiral Michaelis: No. However, it was an unusual thing in my family: there was no military in my family, but my sister ended up in the military, and so did I. Upon graduation from college she married a man named Jorgenson, who eventually retired as a colonel in the Marine Corps. So suddenly there was a generation of Michaelises who went into the military where there had been none for many generations. In fact, I think my maternal grandfather came to the United States more than anything else to avoid conscription into the German Army under the Kaiser during the First World War.

My career at the Naval Academy from 1936 to 1940 was during the Depression years.

---

[*] The Navy instituted the aviation cadet program in 1935. Individuals enlisted in the Naval Reserve, then were trained as aviators and sent to the fleet before being commissioned as officers. In 1939 the program was modified so that individuals were commissioned upon successful completion of flight training.

Q: From whom did you get your appointment to the Naval Academy?

Admiral Michaelis: The congressman from Kansas City. My maternal grandfather was very instrumental in convincing this cohort of his that he should send me to the Naval Academy. My grandfather was very much opposed to my attending the Naval Academy. It wasn't until he saw that I kept up the same persistence for two years that he decided he would help me. He felt that the military in all its forms was terribly undemocratic. For instance, the officers ate separately from the enlisted men. So he was determined that, for at least a reasonable period of time, he would try to talk me out of doing anything military.

It was a difficult decision to make. During the Depression I was working while I was going to high school in the summer times. I was working for a grain commission house in Kansas City, the Scholar-Bishop Grain Company, the main stockholder of the company being a Mr. Bishop. When he found out I had received an appointment, he suggested that he pay the rest of my way to university for the next two years. Then I would come to the company, and he would assure me a seat on the Board of Trade within three years after I graduated.

Q: What a temptation.

Admiral Michaelis: That was a big temptation.

Q: Did you get any assistance from your family in this?

Admiral Michaelis: No, they left it entirely up to me, but in their secret heart I feel they would like to have had me stay at home. However, I looked at a lot of the people who had spent their whole lives in the grain business, in and out of the grain pits. I decided I wanted to spend my time a little differently than to be a grain trader for the rest of my life. That was the only inhibiting influence at the time I went to the Naval Academy.

Q: It was a mighty big problem for a young man to struggle with.

Admiral Michaelis: It was indeed. I think possibly had he not been so late in making that offer, and had I not had my heart set on the academy for so long, I might not have fulfilled the appointment.

Q: And you would be trading with the Russians today.

Admiral Michaelis: That's right. I think I was subject to the same influences that everybody else was at that time. We were just struggling to get out of the Great Depression. My family, like most others, had been very badly hit--to their great economic detriment. My father spent the last years of his life in very poor health, and I think it could be attributed to the terrible things the Depression did to him and to so many people. While it was doing terrible things to my family, it was my salvation, as it was the first time I realized that I was going to have to get out and do something.

Q: Tell me about your two years at the junior college. What did they contribute to your eventual success at the academy?

Admiral Michaelis: I think they gave me a lot of preparation I wouldn't have had otherwise. I had had a mediocre time in high school, as I had no inclination to do well academically. I had to change around when I decided to go to the Naval Academy; that had to be inverted, so I worked very, very hard in the college. Fortunately, it was a factory; it was not the kind of school you go to and where there were great outside activities with this team and that team and so forth. It was in the downtown district of Kansas City, and it was expected that people who went there would assume the study habits and rules of the factory and achieve something academically.

Q: Was that in the early days of the junior college as an institution?

Admiral Michaelis: Later on that junior college became a part of the University of Kansas City. I don't think today there exists under that name a Junior College of Kansas City.

Q: Were you interested in athletics during your high school days?

Admiral Michaelis: All the way through high school I was much more interested in athletics than I was in academics. I really don't regret that choice at all, because I think making certain athletic teams, at a time when I knew it was going to be very difficult to do so, had really quite a sizable influence--knowing that you can establish certain goals, and if you work hard enough at them, you have a pretty good chance of getting there, even though you may not be the most talented in that particular line.

Q: And then the element of teamwork.

Admiral Michaelis: The element of teamwork, the element of perseverance. As long as it's legal and moral, I don't think what you persevere in as a young person makes too much difference, as long as you learn the value of perseverance and working with your associates in a meaningful teamwork way.
 So I went to the Naval Academy.

Q: How were you impressed with it at first--the military discipline and that kind of thing?

Admiral Michaelis: On the first Saturday night I was sitting in my room writing a letter home, and it suddenly occurred to me that I was in the wrong place, that that was not the way to spend Saturday night.

Q: And you were not permitted to go out on the town.

Admiral Michaelis: It was considerably different than the way it is now. But all in all I think I really had a great appreciation for what the Naval Academy was attempting to do. Like most things at that particular stage of life, I think I got more benefit out of it in retrospect than I did at the instant of application of the disciplines that were imposed at the Naval Academy.

Q: Did you have problems with any of the courses?

Admiral Michaelis: I had a lot of problems doing as well as I would have liked to have done, and I never did. I never had any problems where I was flunking courses. I had my ups and downs, but all I had to do was to think about missing Christmas leave or something--it was so infrequent getting outside of those four gray walls--it was a great motivation not to have to stay around there.

Q: About twice a year wasn't it? How was plebe summer?

Admiral Michaelis: Great. I enjoyed plebe summer.* It was active. It sowed the first seeds of a much bigger picture than I had ever been in before. I could see that the competition was going to be keen and that teamwork was important. I rather enjoyed plebe summer, probably more than I did plebe year.

Q: Obviously you didn't mind the Annapolis summer heat. Coming from Kansas City, I guess it didn't make much difference.

Admiral Michaelis: That's right. Whose humidity would you rather put up with, Maryland's or Missouri's?

---

* A first-year midshipman is known as a plebe. The first part of his indoctrination to the Naval Academy occurs during plebe summer.

There were no prizes at the Naval Academy. I earned no varsity letters. I was sort of muscle fodder for the wrestling team. I played plebe football and probably had a pretty good opportunity to move on there, but I had a tremendous amount of trouble with one knee. After it was operated on, it was recommended that I give up football and not play it anymore.

Q: What was it, an injury playing football?

Admiral Michaelis: Yes, it was an injury playing football. It was one of these instances where you can't put your finger on exactly where it happened. But whatever started it, it kept getting worse.

Q: Was a bone dislodged? You mentioned an operation.

Admiral Michaelis: It was to some degree. But this was the other one. I have had three operations on the knee.

I was not too much in the academics. I was in the upper fourth of my class but just barely. My class was a small one; about 440 people graduated, and my number was 100.[*] So I just made the upper fourth.

Q: Who was superintendent at that time?

Admiral Michaelis: It was Jerry Wright.[†]

Q: He was a tough taskmaster, wasn't he.

---

[*] Midshipman Michaelis stood 100th of the 456 graduates in the Naval Academy class of 1940.
[†] Commander Jerauld Wright, USN, was a battalion officer at the Naval Academy from 1939 to 1941. The superintendents at the time were Rear Admiral David F. Sellers, USN, 1934-38, and Rear Admiral Wilson Brown, USN, 1938-41.

Admiral Michaelis: Yes. We thought a lot of him--at least I did--though we were much more distant from the superintendent than it seems to me the midshipmen are today. At least when my boy was going through the academy they seemed to be considerably closer to the superintendent.* But that may not have been the case. It may have just been an impression I had because the superintendents were closer to my peers than they were when I was a midshipman.

If I were to describe my stay at the Naval Academy, it was somewhat lackluster. There were not many of the attributes--I should say of the sort of add-ons--at the Naval Academy in those days in which people blossomed forth. There was an absolute minimum of funds; every dollar was carefully spent. It was a very, very difficult time for doing anything with public funds except to spend them on non-glamorous things. We were fortunate at that time, I think, to have had a good plant at the Naval Academy. I believe if the Depression had come on 15 years before, they might have had some trouble.

Q: I've seen pictures of that.

Did you have an aviation summer?

Admiral Michaelis: Yes, we did. Each of us had a flight and did a little navigating. We were taken over for an indoctrination ride in the little "Yellow Perils."† One ride each. We did not go anyplace like Norfolk or anyplace where we could observe any real squadron life or anything of this nature.

Q: Did it whet your appetite?

Admiral Michaelis: It reinforced it. It was there.

---

* Frederick H. Michaelis, Jr., graduated from the Naval Academy in the class of 1969.
† "Yellow Peril" was the nickname for the yellow-painted N3N trainer, a biplane equipped with a centerline pontoon. It was 26 feet long, had a wing span of 34 feet, gross weight of 2,792 pounds, and a top speed of 126 miles per hour.

I had a very discouraging thing happen when I left the Naval Academy. For reasons that I don't understand, my eyes had deteriorated. I graduated on a temporary two-year commission, which, if I didn't bring my eyes up, I had the opportunity of leaving the Navy or going into the Supply Corps.

Q: Neither one of which was very inviting.

Admiral Michaelis: I think I would have left the Navy.

Q: How did you build them up again?

Admiral Michaelis: I didn't build them up; they just built up. One of the times when I went into the hospital with a knee problem, I rested my eyes and so forth. I think it was just strain and the bad lamps at the Naval Academy.

Then in January 1941, before the war started, everybody--regardless of his taste--had to take a flight physical. In case there was a war, they wanted to have a list of people that they could call on.

Q: The need then became apparent for fliers.

Admiral Michaelis: Yes, that they could shanghai if necessary into aviation. Without thinking there was any chance of passing my eye examination, I took the examination, and I passed it.

Q: You hadn't memorized the chart?

Admiral Michaelis: No. I couldn't believe it, and I really didn't want to believe that it wasn't true. I didn't want to be a flier if I was going to be a halfhearted flier and if I really couldn't see. I took three examinations, and I asked for the second and third. For the last one I stayed up most of the night and went to a movie. I did all the things that in those days were considered to be bad for your eyes. I sat way over on the side in the movie, did all those things you could possibly think of. This was sort of a juvenile thing to do, but I really was quite concerned. I wanted to see well if I was going to fly. I passed the third examination, so I put in for aviation immediately.

Q: In those days I think they had a system of eye exercises at the academy. Did you get involved in that?

Admiral Michaelis: No. I think that probably you could have gotten into that if you went after it. But it wasn't until three months before I graduated that I knew I was going to have a temporary commission. And I had taken a second examination before they made this decision. I must not have been too far below the cutoff point.

Q: What about the summer cruises? They were somewhat curtailed at that point.

Admiral Michaelis: Our first summer cruise was excellent. We had a good cruise. We went to Funchal, Madeira. Then we proceeded on up the coast and went through the Kiel Canal in Germany, bumping our way among the battleships all the way. I took four days in Berlin, which was a most interesting time. That was 1937, and I guess it seemed to me that at least one-quarter of the people were in uniform of varying hues and colors: blacks, browns, and boots and so forth.

Q: Hitler was completely in the saddle?*

Admiral Michaelis: Yes, he was, but Berlin was the same gay place that it had been up until that time--lots of attractions for visitors. We went back around through the Kattegat to the separation of the Skagerrak between Sweden and Denmark. That was a fine cruise, and I

---

* Adolf Hitler was Chancellor of Germany from 1933 until his death in 1945.

think we got a lot of training; that was my youngster cruise.* We were still sleeping in hammocks at the time, the upper classmen sleeping in cots. I remember that clearly. I thought hammock sleeping was great.

Q: Were you coaling the ship?

Admiral Michaelis: We didn't coal; we were oil-fired. It was the Wyoming. In my first class cruise I was in the New York, a battleship. Everybody wanted to go to the New York in those days, because she was a much better feeder.

Q: That was a legitimate incentive.

Admiral Michaelis: First-class cruise was coastal; the farthest away from the U.S. was Nova Scotia.

Q: Now because of the imminence of war?

Admiral Michaelis: Yes, we went to Halifax. This was in '39, and I graduated in '40. It was the first class to have our leave curtailed, and we got to our ships. The scent of war was in the air; there wasn't any doubt about it.

Q: Did you have a choice of your ship?

Admiral Michaelis: I could only get a surface ship, couldn't get a carrier. So I opted for the biggest surface ship, because it had navigation aboard. I went to a battleship, the Pennsylvania; I first was assistant navigator.† Then I became a battery officer in their

---

* The "youngster" or third-class year at the Naval Academy is the equivalent of the sophomore year at a civilian university.
† The USS Pennsylvania (BB-38) was commissioned 12 June 1916. Following modernization in the early 1930s she had a standard displacement of 33,384 tons, was 608

secondary battery, which was a surface battery of 5-inch guns, which were always in the shadow of the big 14-inch guns.

Q: Were there many of your classmates on board?

Admiral Michaelis: Thirteen of us went aboard at the same time. Then, shortly before Pearl Harbor was attacked, I was called in by the exec one day, and he said, "I have a letter here from the Bureau of Navigation." In those days that was the name for the Bureau of Personnel.

Q: Headed by Admiral Nimitz at that point, was it not?*

Admiral Michaelis: Nimitz, yes. This was in the middle of 1941, June or July.

Q: Yes, he was plucked from that to go to Pearl Harbor.

Admiral Michaelis: This message described a radar officer. They were looking for a very stellar, fine-performing individual. The exec said, "The captain and I decided that you would be the radar officer."
    I said, "I'm flattered. Commander, could you tell me what a radar is?"
    He said, "I was afraid you were going to ask that."

Q: It was too secret for him to tell you?

---

feet long and 106 feet in the beam. Her top speed was 21 knots. She was armed with 12 14-inch guns and 12 5-inch/51 broadside guns and eight 5-inch/25 antiaircraft guns.
* Rear Admiral Chester W. Nimitz, USN, who in December 1941 became Commander in Chief Pacific Fleet following the Japanese attack on Pearl Harbor.

Admiral Michaelis: It really was. It was an interesting experience. Then I said, "It wouldn't happen to be that rack that I saw on the 'Prune Barge'? That was what we called the California in those days.

He said, "Yes, I think so." There were only two ships in the fleet that had radar at that time. The old CXAM-1 was a whale of a good radar for its time, and I don't think anything touched it for about three or four models after that.[*] It had the old A-scan type of presentation. The two ships that had radar were the Chester, a cruiser, and the California. So I went out for a few days on the Chester to find out all the lore about radar. In those days it was really the halt leading the blind.

Shortly after that, maybe two weeks, I signed for a tremendous amount of gear coming aboard while we were in the yard there at Pearl. We put this thing together, and I signed for it, not having any idea what I was signing for. My hide was literally saved by a chief radioman named Klouck, who was absolutely the most amazing radioman.[†] He not only knew the operation of radio, but he knew about the guts of radio. Once you know radio and understand the principle of radar, you become a pretty good radarman. He had never been to MIT or any of the rest of the technical schools. He was self-taught and really made the thing hum.

It was an interesting thing. We had a servo in this little shack. He used to crank a very small dial, and the radar face would swing around, and you could read the azimuth. It was always relative, so you had to convert it to true.[‡] You would keep cranking it until you could see a blip out on this long skinny tube. It was called an A-tube, and you had to calibrate it almost every day. It was calibrated in thousandths and tens of thousandths of yards out on this tube. When you would see a blip on there, you would stop. You would read the angle, and then you would go out on the tube and read the distance, and then you would plot a point on a piece of paper.

---

[*] The CXAM was an early air-search radar.
[†] Chief Radioman Charles H. Klouck, USN, who later became an officer and eventually retired as a lieutenant commander.
[‡] This is a reference to the bearings of a given object in relation to the ship.

Q: Very primitive.

Admiral Michaelis: It really was; it was an interesting thing.

Q: About that time I believe one of your colleagues, Rivero, was learning in the department about radar. He became the chief radar man without any prior knowledge.[*]

Admiral Michaelis: It was interesting that during the peace days before the war, late 1941, my classmates used to call down from the bridge when they had the deck. They would say, "What do you have on the port bow?" I would crank it around and couldn't find anything, and they would say, "Why don't you throw that piece of junk away? There's a ship out there."

I would say, "Can you see the running lights or just the truck light?"[†]

They would say, "Just the truck light."

I would say, "Well, it's hull down, and I told you there has got to be something for these radar signals to bounce off of."

I never convinced them until the war started and we started steaming dark. I was the most popular man aboard ship at that point, including the captain, because I really had some eyes. We ran right through a convoy one night before the captain was convinced that he must either change course or turn on lights or something. He turned on lights, and that whole convoy turned on lights, and we were running right down through the middle of them. I had been telling the captain for 25,000 yards that we were running into a gaggle of ships.

Also, at Pearl Harbor at one time the Pennsylvania's radar was the only one that was out there. For about 40 hours after the attack on Pearl we had the guard and were hooked

---

[*] Lieutenant Horacio Rivero, Jr., USN, was then assigned to the Bureau of Ordnance in the Navy Department. The oral history of Rivero, who retired as a four-star admiral, is in the Naval Institute collection.

[†] The red truck lights are at the very top of the ship and thus would be the first things visible as a ship began to appear over the horizon.

up by telephone lines to the control center. We could call our plots in to them in a very crude manner.

Q: In retrospect you must have proved your mettle prior to being selected as a radar officer. What characteristics were predominant that caused them to choose you?

Admiral Michaelis: I really think they were simply the kind of adjectives that would convince a young man that it was important for him to take on this job when he knew nothing about it. It really didn't describe anything that would say anything. None of the description had anything to do with technical capabilities, because nobody had any technical training. It simply was this: they wanted to get somebody that they felt secure about his ability to keep his mouth shut and try to learn something and make it applicable to the ship. I worked very hard during those days. I really felt that it was a monumental breakthrough, and it turned out to be.

Q: There was very little printed material then.

Admiral Michaelis: Very little. And, you know, that radar was good enough. I look back on that with a great deal of surprise. If I happened to be getting around to the right sector to detect airplanes as well as ships, I could follow a 14-inch shell as long as I was training right down the line of gunfire from my own ship. I could spot with it, though I couldn't see the target that well. It was an interesting period in my life. I had the opportunity later on to try to teach relative motion to some Army Air Corps people who were being trained as ground control officers.* Relative motion was a lot harder for them than it was for the Navy people.

Q: I can see that.

---

* On 20 June 1941 the U.S. Army Air Corps was officially redesignated the U.S. Army Air Forces.

Admiral Michaelis: It really was. You know, in an airplane sensing relative motion of another airplane is sort of second nature. But where you have got to plot it and steer it on a relative line and so forth, it was difficult. So that was a very busy time for me for, I guess several weeks before we were fixed up and left Pearl.

Q: Was the Pennsylvania operating in the Pacific from the time you joined her? Was she a part of the Pacific Fleet?

Admiral Michaelis: Yes, she was. She was home-ported in Long Beach and had long ago had sort of an ersatz home port in Pearl Harbor. The fleet left the West Coast in 1940 and never really came back.[*]

Q: That was under the influence of Admiral Richardson.

Admiral Michaelis: Yes. Admiral Richardson, of course, tried to get them out of there.[†] He flew his flag in the Pennsylvania, and Admiral Kimmel followed him.[‡] Richardson made a secret trip to the United States, back to Washington, to try to get the battleships out of death-trap row. It seemed to me that with the exception of two or three differences--somewhat minor--that the Japanese planned their attack right down the pattern that he had prognosticated many months before the attack on Pearl Harbor.

An interesting thing happened aboard the ship. I was at my sister's house until the first word on the radio, and I got to my ship.

Q: She was living where?

---

[*] In the spring of 1940 the U.S. Fleet's Battle Force left California to take part in Fleet Problem XXI in the Hawaiian Islands. Because of the worsening international situation, President Franklin D. Roosevelt elected to keep the warships in Hawaiian waters rather than permitting them to return to their West Coast bases as scheduled.
[†] Admiral James O. Richardson, USN, served as Commander in Chief U.S. Fleet from January 1940 to February 1941.
[‡] Admiral Husband E. Kimmel, USN, served as Commander in Chief Pacific Fleet from February to December in 1941.

Admiral Michaelis: Kaimokee, right in Honolulu. Her husband had the Marine detachment on a cruiser that was out at sea.* When I got back to the ship, I found that a bomb had gone through my stateroom, and I thought my roommate, who had the duty, was aboard. I tried to put that out of my mind but couldn't. It was a tremendous thing that about noontime that day I saw him come down the passageway. I had been really afraid to ask anybody whether they had seen Chuck Beers, my roommate, so it was fortunate that neither of us had been in the room when the bomb hit.†

Q: You were on shore?

Admiral Michaelis: I was on shore at the time the attack started. When the second wave started, I was back aboard.

Q: How did you get back to the ship?

Admiral Michaelis: I got in my car and really got the jump on the crowd. I had gone to sleep with the radio on over my head. I don't know what aroused me, but it must have been the strident announcements being made on the radio. I got up and had a drive that was normally about 22-25 minutes; I cut that time considerably. The crowd of cars hadn't really started forming until I got near the gate where they were converging.

Q: What was the damage to the Pennsylvania?

Admiral Michaelis: The damage was fairly light. We got hit with about four bombs; I think it was four. The Cassin and the Downes were two destroyers that were in the dry dock ahead of us, and they were badly damaged. They pasted both of them back together, and

---

* Captain Kenneth A. Jorgensen, USMC, commanded the Marine detachment of the heavy cruiser Northampton (CA-26).
† Ensign Charles J. Beers, USN.

the Downes came back to the United States with a concrete bow.* The dock was flooded as soon as the attack started, of course. The first lieutenant was killed on the pier while he was in charge of having the dock flooded. The damage to the Pennsylvania was not heavy.

Q: Did you have any casualties on board?

Admiral Michaelis: Yes, there were casualties. In fact, there were a couple of gun casemates. That was what they used to call those heavy metal doors that swung back so the gun was exposed. Any bomb going off inside the casemate pretty well finished anybody in the casemate, and we had a couple of gun crews that were killed to the man. Burned their clothes off and dismembered them in many cases. Not a very pleasant cleanup job, but we were a lot better off than many of the other ships.

We got under way maybe ten days after the attack, and the word was that we were going to shift berths. I had gone out to my car, and persons unknown had put an ice pick through all four of my tires. I assumed it was part of that Japanese group that reportedly did quite a bit of damage. In any event, I was laboriously taking them off and running them one at a time up to the garage. The chaplain came out and said, "We're going to shift berths." So I left the tools lying on the seat and the car up on jacks and went aboard ship. I hadn't been aboard very long when I realized you didn't do the preparations that were being made if you were going to shift berths. I don't think there were more than half a dozen officers who knew we were going to get under way. It is interesting how well they could keep secrets in those days.†

Q: In contrast with today.

---

* For details, see John D. Alden, "Up from Ashes--The Saga of Cassin and Downes, U.S. Naval Institute Proceedings, January 1961, pages 32-41. According to Alden's article, remaining portions of the two destroyers came back to the West Coast on board other ships rather than in their own hulls.
† The Pennsylvania left Pearl Harbor on 20 December 1941 and steamed to San Francisco, where she arrived on the 29th.

Admiral Michaelis: It was the business of everybody deciding this thing was bigger than their own personal need for peer status and recognition and so forth.

So we then went back to Hunters Point and got some guns put aboard and so forth. By that time I had put in for flight training.

Q: You had indicated this well before, however?

Admiral Michaelis: Yes, and the captain of the ship was very desirous of my not going to flight training. He thought it was really best for myself and for his command that I stay aboard.

Q: Because of your radar proficiency?

Admiral Michaelis: Everybody who had just a little experience was considered important in the command. They had lost many people who were put aboard new construction and so forth. In the captain's view, anybody that was going to waste his time going into flight training was much more badly needed where he was.

Q: Was that still the point of view that prevailed that long?

Admiral Michaelis: Oh, very strong in those days.

Q: Aviation training for young fellows was a bad word.

Admiral Michaelis: As it was, we had to wait two years for it. So I got back very late in 1942, almost 1943. Then I went to flight training.

Q: How was your time spent in San Francisco? You went there for repairs.

Admiral Michaelis: Learning a lot about radar. Learning about gun-laying radar.* We got the first gun-laying radar for the 5-inch/25 guns they put aboard us.

Q: Was there any relaxing of the secrecy about radar at that point?

Admiral Michaelis: No, not very much. I think it was very closely held. I don't believe I was in a position really to know how many people knew about radar, but I will tell you they were pretty careful with the numbers of people aboard the ship that knew about radar.

When we went to sea after that, we steamed out with a whole bunch of battleships. We went on what was really a diversionary force for the Battle of Midway.† Remember when they made that swing up to Dutch Harbor? We didn't get to Dutch Harbor, but we were part of a sizable diversionary force.

An interesting aviation problem happened at that time, and I'll never forget it as long as I live. I guess we had an OS2U up from every one of the battleships.‡ The senior aviator up reported a fog bank ahead. Then he reported it again. Finally, he said, "You'd better do something about it." In the meantime, we were getting all our signals up on the flag hoist, and we were all going to turn around together in formation for a cast recovery.§

Q: This was up in the Aleutians?

---

* Typically this is referred to as fire-control radar in the U.S. Navy. "Gun-laying" is more a British term.
† For a brief discussion of this deployment, see Samuel Eliot Morison, Coral Sea, Midway and Submarine Actions: May 1942-August 1942 (Boston: Little, Brown, 1949), pages 82-83.
‡ The Vought OS2U Kingfisher was the principal floatplane used by U.S. battleships and cruisers in World War II for scouting and spotting the fall of shot. It was 34 feet long, had a wing span of 36 feet, gross weight of 6,000 pounds, and maximum speed of 164 miles an hour. It was armed with two .30-caliber machine guns.
§ "Cast," which was a letter in the phonetic alphabet of the time, designated a recovery method whereby the airplane landed on the water, rode up on a sea sled, and was lifted aboard by a crane on the ship's fantail.

Admiral Michaelis: Yes, the Aleutians, and we played a real havoc getting those planes back aboard. Because about the time we were in the middle of the turn, we were suddenly in the middle of the fog, and one plane crashed into the mast of one of the ships. We got them all aboard except the one that crashed and one that landed on the water. Several of them landed on the water, but one was pretty far away. Remember those old radio direction-finders? We got him back aboard, but by that time we had given our position away, because we had come up on high-frequency radio to save this fellow.

Q: Was the Pennsylvania at that time involved in a simple kind of amphibious operation up there?

Admiral Michaelis: I guess we were supposed to act as a diversionary force, but I never did really understand this. We were not to get in close enough to be brought under attack.

After we came back from that, we returned to San Francisco. Shortly thereafter, I left the ship and went to New Orleans for primary flight training.

Q: That was in October 1942.

Admiral Michaelis: Yes, it was, though it seemed it was Christmastime about the time I started flight training.

Q: It was Christmas to you because you were going into aviation.

Admiral Michaelis: Right. I met my wife in New Orleans, and a year later we were married there.

Q: Is New Orleans where you went first for training?

Admiral Michaelis: At the naval air station there. It was then right on Lake Pontchartrain. It is part of the university now. Then I went to Pensacola, then to Melbourne, Florida, for my advanced training in fighters.

Q: Tell me a little about each place and the kind of training at each point.

Admiral Michaelis: It was highly concentrated. We flew from the first rays of light in the morning until the last rays at night at Lake Pontchartrain and also at Pensacola, though it was more concentrated in Pensacola. We went through about three fields down there. As soon as you got certification from having completed one squadron, the next day you reported in, wasting no time, and got checked out for the next phase of flight training. I was finished and got my wings by about May 1943.

Q: What chance did you have for romance when you were so busy?

Admiral Michaelis: It was like everything else; it was very concentrated.

I think the highlight of that period was qualifying in F4Fs on the Wolverine up in the Great Lakes.* It was a converted side-wheel lake steamer that they put a couple of wires on. We flew out of the naval air station at Glenview, Illinois, and landed aboard the Wolverine. We did six landings, and we were qualified.

Q: Did you have any problems? Did you have any downs during the course of training?

Admiral Michaelis: I had a terrible problem. They were soloing you as soon as you were ready--a grand total of seven hours before you soloed. But if you were ready at five, which I was, then you soloed. I really thought I was an ace already. I came back to the field, and, of course, in those days there was no radio. They were all gosports, and you used your

---

* Grumman F4F Wildcat fighters first entered fleet squadrons in 1940. The F4F-4 was 29 feet long, wing span of 38 feet, gross weight of 7,952 pounds, and top speed of 318 miles per hour. It was armed with six .50-caliber machine guns.

eyes and looked at the lights in the tower, the flags flying, or whatever it may be. You looked where the wind sock was, and they had a traffic indicator for which direction you were landing. When the flights were over, you would have people landing three or four abreast.

When I came in to land, there was an instructor who had come up on my right wing. When he and I landed, our wingtips collided. So on my solo flight I was charged with an accident involving an instructor. This didn't bode too well. I was incensed, and I never should have been incensed. I should have kept my mouth shut, which I didn't, and from that point on I found I had to do things pretty perfectly. I got a down on my first check ride after that and passed my second check ride; I had my troubles at New Orleans. After that, everything was fine. That was mainly because I had brought it on myself. It was a good thing to have happen.

Q: Perhaps taught you some humility?

Admiral Michaelis: That was a good dose of humility among my peers. It never hurts.

Q: Who were some of your colleagues at that point who became famous as aviators?

Admiral Michaelis: Some were long time famous, not necessarily as aviators. There was Mickey Weisner, who went through at the same time as I did.* I don't know if they were immediately during my time. We had many aviators who made great names for themselves, some fighters who were successful in downing Japanese planes. I will say this--there was a guy who during the Marianas Turkey Shoot knocked down seven airplanes.† He was down

---

* Ensign Maurice F. Weisner, USN, Naval Academy class of 1941. In 1979 Weisner retired as a four-star admiral.
† The "Great Marianas Turkey Shoot" took place on 19 June 1944 while U.S. carriers were supporting the invasion of Saipan. That day U.S. planes shot down more than 300 Japanese aircraft. The highest-scoring U.S. pilot was Commander David McCampbell, USN, air group commander from the carrier Essex (CV-9), who shot down seven Japanese. In 1943 he was on duty at Melbourne, Florida.

there with us; he was an instructor then and went back to the war zone for a second tour.

An unusual thing happened. I knew which air wing I was going to before I ever left Melbourne.

Q: How did that happen?

Admiral Michaelis: Charles Crommelin, who was in my view the pick of the litter among the many fine Crommelins, had convinced somebody along the line that air groups should be formed up with a nucleus of people.[*] They would go down and pick up their squadrons' additional numbers at Pensacola, build up their squadrons, and know their people from their early days. Crommelin's fighter squadron commander was a commander named Noel Gayler.[†] I was Noel Gayler's squadron flight officer first, then his executive officer. I took the squadron from Noel once we were out in the Pacific, VF-12.

Q: What kind of training was given at Melbourne?

Admiral Michaelis: Fighter training, and I remained there as instructor for six months. That was the mode for people who were lieutenants and didn't have much flight time. They knew they were going to be squadron commanders fairly early on, and they needed buildups and experience so they could spend a little time leading their squadron rather than learning to fly. It was really a fine idea. We were terribly impatient to get out of there, but there were better heads than ours that kept us down there. We became pretty good gunners, and we were instructing in aerial combat.

Q: Like everybody else, you wanted to get out into the fray, even though you were doing a job where you were.

---

[*] Commander Charles L. Crommelin, USN, Commander Carrier Air Group 12 in the Randolph (CV-15). He was one five brothers who served in the war as naval officers.
[†] Commander Noel A. M. Gayler, USN. The oral history of Gayler, who retired as a four-star admiral, is in the Naval Institute collection.

Admiral Michaelis: So we took the Randolph out for her first combat duty. She had just been commissioned.*

Q: Who was her skipper?

Admiral Michaelis: Felix Baker, who retired as a captain.† I thought he was a good captain.

Q: He fell into disfavor with somebody, didn't he?

Admiral Michaelis: Yes, he did, somewhere along the line. I never knew what it was.

Q: He had qualifications for flag.

Admiral Michaelis: He was a good, solid, hard-living guy. he was cool.

Q: I think Charlie Minter talked about him.‡

Admiral Michaelis: That's right, Charlie and I were shipmates. That's where I met Charlie Minter. Charlie was then--and has been since--one of the most outstanding persons I have ever known. When you speak of people that you have a great appreciation for and that you like to be around, he fills that bill for me.

---

* The USS Randolph (CV-15) was commissioned 9 October 1944. She had a displacement of 36,380 tons, was 888 feet long, 93 feet in the beam, an extreme width of 148 feet on the flight deck, and had a draft of 29 feet. She had a top speed of 32 knots and could accommodate about 90 planes.
† Captain Felix L. Baker, USN, commanded the USS Randolph (CV-15) from October 1944 to July 1945.
‡ Vice Admiral Charles S. Minter, Jr., USN (Ret.), is the subject of a Naval Institute oral history that discusses his World War II service in the Randolph.

Interview Number 2 with Admiral Frederick H. Michaelis, U.S. Navy (Retired)

Place: Naval Historical Center, Washington, D.C.

Date: Thursday, 19 November 1981

Interviewer: John T. Mason, Jr.

Q: You resume the story at the point where you are going out to the Pacific. Did you get into the conflict?

Admiral Michaelis: Actually, during the intervening period between May or June 1944 and the turn of the year, 1945, we spent at various training places--mainly up in Astoria, Oregon, at Clatsop County Airport. The air group was broken up and the various squadrons sent to different places. The fighter squadron was up there for a while. That merely puts the beginning of the tour in the Pacific at about the beginning of 1945. The interesting thing about this particular tour was that it was the ship's first entry. She was a new ship, the Randolph.

Q: Had the crew been trained?

Admiral Michaelis: The crew had been trained in the carrier training system. I guess some 10% or 12% of the people aboard, maybe a little more than that, were seasoned old-timers. Maybe another 10% had had some experience before they went into training. The rest of the crew was composed of people who were in the recruit-plus category.

    The second thing that was interesting was that our very first taste of combat was in the initial attacks on the homeland of Japan.*

Q: This was in February?

---

* During his time in VF-12 in the Randolph, Michaelis was flying an F6F Hellcat.

Admiral Michaelis: February of 1945.

Q: Were you dropping fire bombs or what?

Admiral Michaelis: No, we didn't go after the cities; we were after military targets at that time. My first strike was on the Koizumi airframe plant in the Tokyo area, and the second one was against an airfield. We had very little opposition.

We went in under interesting weather conditions. There was an inversion at the coastline: good weather over the targets and terrible weather out over the ship. That went on for a couple of days, making strikes.[*] Then we retired and went back to Ulithi.[†] Ulithi was our stopping point on the way out. We went back to Ulithi, and after a few days there we went up to support the invasion of Iwo Jima.

Q: How do you account for the lack of opposition over the Japanese mainland?

Admiral Michaelis: We got opposition. First of all, we struck with 14 carriers, and that is a very formidable group of aircraft. The first day was a matter of surprise. The second day there was more opposition, but a great many of the airplanes had been shifted south to Kyushu, and you will recall in '44 with the big air activities in the Philippines.

Q: At that point didn't they have a tendency to conserve?

Admiral Michaelis: They did after that Philippine Sea "turkey shoot;" the Japanese had lost an awful lot of airplanes. More difficult than that for them was the beginning of their lack of fuel for training their new pilots. So their pilot replacement was coming much slower than it should at the time.

---

[*] These strikes were on 16-17 February 1945.
[†] Actually, Task Force 58 went directly to Iwo Jima to support the U.S. invasion that took place on 19 February.

Q: Did you feel Admiral Radford's influence?

Admiral Michaelis: Yes, indeed. He was a most remarkable man.

My first introduction to Radford was while we were still out on the line after our first attacks on Tokyo. I got summoned over to his flagship.* I didn't realize that he personally read those combat reports that we had written. I had made a very slighting comment about a situation when I had lost a pilot. I had flown over, and he had gotten in his raft and was in a place where I thought a submarine should come in and pick him up. It turned out that it was a minefield, so when I made these castigating remarks about the failure of the rescue service, I found myself strapped into an airplane and went over and landed on the ship that Admiral Radford had his flag on. I saw him personally about this, and he told me that they looked after the pilots very well. If I didn't know where the minefields were, I had better put some trust and faith in the fact that they did, and they knew what limitations they had. But he also listened.

I said, "You know, there was nothing that told us that was a minefield there. With the pilot going down into the water, he ought to know that he is landing in a minefield."

He said, "There's a great compromise between the kinds of exchange of intelligence that have to take place." And he let it go at that. He is a great follow-up man.

Q: Do you want to say something at this point about the rescue operations in World War II?

Admiral Michaelis: They were generally fine. They effected rescues with having given very little initial thought as to how to do this in time of war. They used whatever they had: submarines, surface ships, patrol boats.

Q: So much of it had to be on the spur of the moment.

---

* In early 1945, Rear Admiral Arthur W. Radford, USN, commanded Task Group 58.1 with his flag in the carrier Yorktown (CV-10).

Admiral Michaelis: It did. What I am saying is that many of us thought that the real heroes of the war--if there were any--were the people who were responsible for rescuing pilots or for rescuing anybody else. I flew top cover over a torpedo plane crew in the Inland Sea and some attacks we made on Kyushu, and one against an airfield at Usa. (That was the comment that people made--that all the toys and so forth that came from Japan were shipped from Usa, "made in Usa.") We had two pilots in the water, and the cover kept moving away ships that were coming toward them until the OS2Us could get there.

This actually happened. Two OS2Us landed, and there were three people from a torpedo plane to be picked up. They got one of them in the cockpit of one OS2U and two in the other cockpit, one on top of the other. They used cartridge starters in those days to start the engines. The second airplane was supposed to take off, but the engine died on him on the first attempt. This was the heavy plane, and he was out of cartridges. The other plane, which had already taken off, beautifully made a circle, came down and landed, and cut his engine. The pilot got out on the spar of the plane and took a line from the other one, then pulled him close enough to hand him four or five cartridges. Then they both started their engines and got away. That second plane stayed on the water until he burned out enough fuel to represent the weight of the second man he had picked up. Fortunately, the weather conditions were good. But they did an amazing thing. They were absolutely fearless in the types of things they did to make rescues.

Q: As a footnote to that, Moorer told me one time that he thought the rescue operations in Vietnam were the most exciting and impressive parts of the whole operation.*

Admiral Michaelis: It has always been, somehow or other--in the last three conflicts we have had, starting with World War II and coming forward--I think the rescue operations have always been good. They have been unsung, really, except for some spasmodic signs of appreciation. It is mainly because they were made up of many, many different parts--not

---

* Admiral Thomas H. Moorer, USN, served as Chief of Naval Operations from 1 August 1967 to 1 July 1970. He was later Chairman of the Joint Chiefs of Staff from 3 July 1970 to 30 June 1974. His oral history is in the Naval Institute collection.

something like would be called the 16th Air Force. It is called the rescue service of the U.S. Navy and is made up of just about everything that can effect a rescue.

Q: That is something that is compelling to human nature very often.

Q: Yes, it is, and people forget all the rules--well, they don't forget them all, but enough to make a rescue. I witnessed a lot of rescues, and the only one I knew of personally in which there was not a rescue attempted was the one that Radford helped me to remember.

Q: And in rather an impressive way.

Admiral Michaelis: Radford was a hard, steely man--I'll tell you.

Q: What was your role in the Iwo Jima operation?

Admiral Michaelis: We mostly supported the ground forces on Iwo Jima. We laid a lot of napalm on the sides of Mount Suribachi at designated targets. It was the first time in wartime experience that I had operated under ground controllers, where we were doing what came to be known as close air support. In my view it worked amazingly well from the very beginning. The accuracy of marking targets was very primeval, but it worked.

Q: Was that a fierce battle for Iwo Jima?

Admiral Michaelis: Yes, it was a fierce battle. We, of course, didn't feel it in the air as much as those on the ground did. At least from talking to the Marines and the soldiers, it seemed to me that every square foot was highly contested--almost the entire island.

Iwo Jima, of course, cleared the way for moving into the Okinawa area.* Okinawa was one of the places where we had not really expected to linger with the fleet so long. We

---

* U.S. forces invaded Okinawa on 1 April 1945.

expected the land-based air to take over a little more rapidly than they did. It was never quite clear to me whether that was slowness in getting organized ashore, which indeed it was, or whether it was our ineptness in making sure that we cleared the way so that they could get solidly established.

Q: Was it due to the ferocity of the Japanese?

Admiral Michaelis: It was a combination of both, and, of course, their defenses were better prepared than we had expected.

Q: It was a bigger island and their last stand, wasn't it?

Admiral Michaelis: It was their last stand. Though we had had a lot of kamikaze efforts earlier on, it was during this time that we really began to get a strange mix of first-line aircraft and kamikazes. Strange because it wasn't always predictable. On the same flight that we encountered a rather sizable air engagement, we came back to the ship and found that two or three kamikazes had gotten through. We were never real sure that the group we encountered and pretty well decimated were intended to be kamikazes or not. They carried no bombs, so I believe they were to be the high air cover. They were all first-line aircraft. They were Georges--aircraft we hadn't seen much of before--and Tonys mainly.* There were no Zeros in that particular group.

Q: But they turned into kamikazes nevertheless?

Admiral Michaelis: No, I don't think they were really intended to be kamikazes. I think they were covering, trying to make sure the kamikazes got in. Only a couple of them did get in. We found them at two levels. We vectored out and found the first level of eight, and then up-sun from them were six more. There were 14 of them, and they did a pretty

---

* The Allies assigned names of men and women to Japanese aircraft so people could speak them quickly without having to struggle with the actual Japanese names.

reasonable job of fighting. We had our hands full. There was a total of six Americans in that engagement. All had success.

I will say one thing in regard to that period in the war. We had some very, very fine people in the early part of the war who did a good job of analyzing what must be done against the Japanese air. There weren't a lot of rules, but you had better follow them; they were good.

Q: Jimmy Thach was one of them.[*]

Admiral Michaelis: Yes, he was and Jimmy Flatley.[†] And we had one of them right with us, Noel Gayler, during the war.[‡] I relieved Noel at Ulithi as squadron commander before we entered our first combat. He went to McCain's staff.[§]

Regarding the rules--and this is something that has been important in every war that I have experienced--it is extremely important to keep up with enemy equipment, no matter what the price. You have to do this in order to be prepared to engage them on terms that are advantageous to your own equipment and your own capabilities. It becomes more important as time goes on, because we have fewer and fewer assets that we can afford to lose at the beginning of a war. Sometimes I have heard some of my confreres say, "We really cannot afford to expend that kind of training effort," and so forth. I have felt strongly, during my time in the Navy, that it was extremely important to have--before the attack--good, realistic adversary-type training and good tactics for penetrating.

Q: We didn't know too much about the Japanese Zero, did we, until we finally caught one

---

[*] Commander John S. Thach, USN. Thach was the inventor of the Thach Weave, a fighter tactic for opposing the Japanese Zeros. His oral history is in the Naval Institute collection.
[†] Commander James H. Flatley, Jr., USN.
[‡] As a lieutenant, Gayler had been in Fighting Squadron Three with Thach at the outset of World War II.
[§] Vice Admiral John S. McCain, USN, was Commander Task Force 38, the fast carrier task force, during the closing months of World War II.

up in the Aleutians?*

Admiral Michaelis: No, we really didn't know. But certainly the training that we had in getting ready for war was valuable. This included flight training from the beginning in various forms, the importance of not doing this and of doing that. Even though we were not yet flying the fighter planes and were still flying the training planes, we got pretty well ground in, and that was extremely valuable. That was something that was done very well during World War II--the emphasis on fundamentals.

By the time we had gotten to Kyushu for making the initial attacks there, Randolph was a seasoned carrier.

Q: Many of our carriers were badly damaged.

Admiral Michaelis: A few were damaged. The Franklin was badly damaged; Enterprise was damaged; and Bunker Hill, right next to us in formation, was hit by two kamikazes. A number of them were damaged to different degrees.

When we came back to Ulithi the second time, we were kamikazied there.† Lying in the atoll, we took a hit by a Frances kamikaze right astern, just at the time when everybody was going to the movies.‡ Fortunately, it was on the stern and not amidships, or there would have been many, many people killed. I think there were just something less than 50 people killed by that particular kamikaze. That was the last time that that ship dropped anchor until we dropped it in Leyte Gulf several months later, and we took a "kamikaze" at that particular time. Only this time it was a U.S. Air Force photographic plane that was making some low passes over there, and he mushed into the deck.

---

* For details see Robert L. Underbrink, "The Day the Navy Caught a Zero," U.S. Naval Institute Proceedings, February 1968, pages 136-137.
† The Randolph was hit by a Japanese kamikaze at 2007 on the evening of 11 March 1945 while anchored at Ulithi Atoll in the Caroline Islands. Casualties included 25 dead and 106 wounded.
‡ "Frances" was the Allied code name for the Japanese P1Y1, a two-engine land-based dive-bombers.

Q: Was there some question about the pilot of that plane?

Admiral Michaelis: There may have been, but I don't recall.

Q: Wasn't it his last flight?

Admiral Michaelis: Yes, it was his last flight.[*] It was an Army photographic P-38.[†] So we dropped the hook only twice, as Charlie Minter has probably mentioned, and we got hit both times.[‡]

Q: That's a lesson in itself.

Admiral Michaelis: Yes, it gives you some idea of our life during that period. We left out there in about June. We had come aboard at the turn of the year, so for six months we dropped anchor twice. We were living at sea.

Q: You are credited with being involved in 20 different attack missions from February to May.

Admiral Michaelis: I know that in the month of April I had what they called "green time," which was combat time. I had a single-seat airplane. I'd have to look at my logbook, but it was over 90 hours, a sizable amount. That was our busiest month, April.

Q: That was the Okinawa climax.

---

[*] The crash killed the Army pilot and several Randolph men.
[†] The P-38 Lightning was a twin-engine fighter plane for the Army Air Forces.
[‡] Vice Admiral Charles S. Minter, USN (Ret.), who was also serving in the Randolph at the time, discussed this incident in his Naval Institute oral history.

Admiral Michaelis: As to the airplanes, everyone was very partial to his own--both the Grumman airplanes, the F6F and the TBF "Turkey," a torpedo plane, and the Chance-Vought F4U. I guess the exception was the SB2C. Too bad that the F8F was never seen by the Japanese. For a propeller plane, it was the finest aerodynamic design for a fighter that we had--but not in time to get into combat.

Q: Would you say something about Admiral Mitscher?[*] He came on board the Randolph as his flagship, didn't he?

Admiral Michaelis: Yes, he did, after the Enterprise was hit. He was ably assisted by two sort of superstars. As a lieutenant commander, I recognized them as superstars, just from my contact with them; that was Arleigh Burke and Jimmy Flatley.[†] They essentially ran the staff activities for Mitscher. Although he was still very active, his health was failing quite rapidly, noticeably. He spent a lot of time sitting in his chair, not moving around like he had in earlier days. There were other very valuable people on that stuff, but those two--Burke and Flatley--ran things mostly.

Q: I think you told me last time that at first you did not know Burke was not a flier.

Admiral Michaelis: From the time they came on the ship until the time I left the ship, I didn't know that he was not a naval aviator. I took problems to him directly, particularly if I couldn't get any satisfaction from the bureaucracy. He gave me carte blanche approval to do things that needed to be done on the spot--things that probably were not realized as to their importance back in the far reaches of Washington. I just assumed that he was a naval aviator; he certainly knew the aviation problems, it seemed to me. He was a good listener.

---

[*] Vice Admiral Marc A. Mitscher, USN, served as Commander Task Force 58, the fast carrier task force.
[†] Commodore Arleigh A. Burke, USN, chief of staff; Commander James H. Flatley, Jr., USN, operations officer.

I left the ship near the end of the war--I guess in July of 1945--and came back for some leave. It was the only time I have ever taken 30 days' leave in my life.

Q: And relished it, I would think, after that.

Admiral Michaelis: I enjoyed it very much, but I was very anxious to get back. The war in Europe was over, but the war in the Pacific was not.

Q: Where did you go on your leave?

Admiral Michaelis: I went back to visit my home and my wife's home. My wife had a baby in the oven when I left, and so I spent a great deal of my time leading the simple life, because she was in the later days of pregnancy.

Q: Was this your son?

Admiral Michaelis: This was my older daughter.
My next duty was to take command of VBF-5, Fighter Bomber Squadron Five. At that time they were stationed in Klamath Falls, Oregon, which was another of those wartime bases at 4,200 feet. In those days it was sometimes hard, with the amount of training the aviators had, or lack of training, to understand the effect of altitude on field operations.

Q: What was the advantage of an air base at that point?

Admiral Michaelis: I don't think there was any advantage at Klamath Falls. It was just another place in the 48 states where they could build a field for training. In many, many places in the country they picked up private fields that were sodded but were in good flat locations in very hilly country. They quickly laid on a training field and put up wooden barrack structures. So it was a matter of taking it where they found it.

Q: The drainage was good, I take it?

Admiral Michaelis: Yes, the drainage was good. Up there I shifted back again to F4Us. I had been flying Hellcats, F6Fs, and we had built a squadron of F4Us. Shortly after, the war was over while I was up there. I continued to command that squadron, and we finally shifted down to the San Diego area.

Q: Did you feel somewhat at loose ends, since the war was over?

Admiral Michaelis: We were spending most of our time doing our part to inform the public of the importance of maintaining an independent status in the Navy. We were flying air shows. I was part of a six-man aerobatics team that I had set up in my squadron; we went to different places. At the same time, we were training, but a great many of the people we had in that squadron were war-tested. They had flown in the war, so the depth of training was less than it would have been if we had been (1) an all-new squadron and (2) going immediately into combat.

To answer your question, we were not at loose ends. We were busy with certain things, with carrying out the various requirements that were placed on us for showing the Navy's wares, which had always been pretty much at sea during the entire war. We were also involved in this transition of people--people leaving, people coming in every day, being undermanned by 20% to 30%.

Q: The point system was taking effect in your area?*

---

* For the demobilization of the U.S. armed forces after World War II, the services had a point system to determine individual priorities for leaving the service. Points were awarded for length of service, overseas service, battle stars, decorations, and dependent children. Those with the highest number of points were the earliest discharged.

Admiral Michaelis: Yes. And we were also very busy trying to maintain the best cream of the crop--trying to keep in the service the pilots with the greatest leadership potential.

Q: What kind of inducements were offered?

Admiral Michaelis: Very few in the beginning. That is one of the things that worked to a great disadvantage shortly after World War II. They developed mainly because of the demands that were coming from the field. Many, many young men were smart enough to see that if they didn't get out and go back to college--a great many of them were high school graduates--they were not going to be competitive in the Navy in a few years. Those were the very people that we wanted, the ones who had that much mental acumen to decide that what they saw ahead was not very fulfilling for them. So I made many trips to my immediate boss, and he sent me back to Washington a couple of times to try to get some of this business of assured selection. It came along but not in due course; it was in very late course.

Q: And it was hard to get the Congress spurred to do things?

Admiral Michaelis: It was hard, and we had such great talent in the armed forces at that time, just by the nature of the numbers of people that were involved and the dedication they had shown. It was an unfortunate lack of foresight. We had done a lot about cleaning people out, getting them back home, as their numbers came up, but we had done very little about the problem of retaining a Navy. Of course, we didn't know what size Navy we wanted.

When I finished up with VBF-5, I left them in Pearl Harbor. They were on their way, and I came back to the United States.

Q: What was their mission to be from that point on?

Admiral Michaelis: They were going out as far as Pearl and no farther. They were going on a training mission, which was the best you could call it at that point. We went out on the Shangri-La.* At that point we hadn't gotten into the commitment for X number of carriers in the Mediterranean and X number of carriers in the Pacific.

I left the ship and went to Postgraduate School.

Q: Was this something you had hoped to do?

Admiral Michaelis: I had put in for it, and frankly I had a lot of misgivings about it. There were many, many interesting things to do. I wasn't sure of my own academic motivations, but I was ordered because I had put in for it several months previously.

Q: But you wanted to stay in the Navy.

Admiral Michaelis: Yes, I had no intention to do other than that. It would have taken wild horses at that point to take me out of the Navy. I was convinced that was one of the best lives anybody could possibly ask for at that stage in life.

I started out at the Postgraduate School in one of the last classes at the Naval Academy.† The Postgraduate School used to be where public works is now.‡ Then I went up to MIT to finish.§

Q: You were enrolled in aeronautical engineering.

Admiral Michaelis: Yes, in a course called "armament," which in those days covered all the basic and advanced aerodynamics and structures and that sort of thing. It was really designed to get a cadre of people who understood advanced dynamics. We were right in

---

* The aircraft carrier Shangri-La (CV-38) was commissioned 15 September 1944.
† Originally established at Annapolis on 9 June 1909, the Naval Postgraduate School was moved to the grounds of the former Hotel Del Monte in Monterey, California, in June 1951.
‡ The building is now known as Halligan Hall.
§ MIT--Massachusetts Institute of Technology.

the beginning of building missiles, and about 1 in 15 was a success. The rest of them were failures, and they were failures mainly because people didn't understand the dynamics of putting together a missile. They built the airframe, and somebody else built the control system, and somebody else built the engine. Then it was all assembled like a Mechano kit, and the dynamic reactions at supersonic speeds were not well understood. When I went to the Postgraduate School at the Naval Academy, I had a professor who proved conclusively to me that no airplane could fly faster than the speed of sound.

Q: And you accepted his thesis?

Admiral Michaelis: Not truly. I remember getting into a couple of positions in airplanes, moving straight down, in which rather unusual things happened to my controls. I realized that there was a transition that had to be made, but I didn't feel that there was a pile-up of air ahead of the wings--a barrier that would keep you from going through if you had enough power and if you had enough strength in the airplane. Now, if you couldn't get both of those in combination, then I would, tentatively at least, accept the theory. There were lots of people in the Navy who believed we were never going to fly faster than the speed of sound. This was in 1946. It was shortly thereafter that the speed of sound was penetrated regularly.[*]

Q: What kind of contact did the PG School have with the Bureau of Ordnance at that point?

Admiral Michaelis: We had very good coordination at the time.

Q: There were people in BuOrd who were working with the idea of missiles then?

---

[*] Flying as a military test pilot, Charles E. Yeager became the first man to exceed the speed of sound on 14 October 1947 in an X-1 rocket.

Admiral Michaelis: There were, but they didn't develop very many successful missiles in that day--1944, 1945, 1946. In 1944 they tried, and they wanted very badly to develop them, but they didn't make it.

It was probably the development of different types of missiles that brought into being the techniques of systems development, instead of component development. This meant developing the entire system, understanding the interactions of all parts of the system--static, dynamic, and so forth--an the understanding of the feedback loops and so forth that had to control such a system.

Q: And the systems management came beside this?

Admiral Michaelis: Systems management followed onto systems development.

Q: And its ultimate development in the Polaris and what followed?[*]

Admiral Michaelis: Yes, the first Air Force Systems Command and the early ballistic missiles were followed on quickly by Red Raborn.[†]

Q: Dan Gallery was involved in that whole thing, too, in the '40s.[‡]

Admiral Michaelis: I am sure he was. I am simply trying to peg this question of the armaments course as being one that was designed to get a better understanding of the systems approach to development.

---

[*] The Polaris submarine-launched ballistic missile system was developed in the late 1950s.
[†] Rear Admiral William F. Raborn, USN, was director of the Special Projects Office, which developed the fleet ballistic missile system. He held the post from 1955 to 1962, being promoted to vice admiral in 1960. His Polaris oral history is in the Naval Institute collection.
[‡] Rear Admiral Daniel V. Gallery, Jr., USN, served as Assistant for Guided Missiles in the Office of the Chief of Naval Operations, 1946-49.

Q: That's why I wondered if they were working in conjunction with BuOrd.

Admiral Michaelis: Yes, in fact, in the summertime we took field trips to various places under the auspices of either BuAer or BuOrd.

Q: What were they doing in Dahlgren at that time?*

Admiral Michaelis: At that time they were still mostly on interior ballistics for guns. There was very little missile work there. There was some computation going on there with the guided missiles. In those days a great deal of computation was pretty hard, before we had digital systems.

Q: You spent one year at Annapolis and two up at MIT?

Admiral Michaelis: I spent nearly two years at Annapolis and a year and a summer at MIT. The summer was to write my thesis at the end.

Q: Under whom did you work during that period at MIT?

Admiral Michaelis: Dr. Stark Draper was my mentor, and I couldn't have found a better, more determined man. He felt he had the secret to control systems and inertial systems, and it turned out he did. At the end of the war, Draper brought a couple of Germans over, and a couple more went down to Huntsville, Alabama. But I think Draper and MIT had the jump on inertial systems.

Q: His efforts came to fruition also in Polaris.†

---

* The Naval Proving Ground for ordnance development was at Dahlgren, Virginia.
† For more on this subject, see the Naval Institute oral history of Vice Admiral Thomas R. Weschler, USN (Ret.), who did postgraduate work under Draper about the same time Michaelis did. Draper was also involved in the guidance systems used for sending men to the moon in the late 1960s.

Admiral Michaelis: Yes, the servo mechanism, which was a new word at that time.

Q: They were developed and current just before World War II, were they not? Ed Hooper was involved in that up at MIT.*

Admiral Michaelis: Yes, but I was never a student of the history of this development. We had as one of Dr. Draper's assistants a man who eventually became Secretary of the Air Force. Draper had some really fine people working up there. I mention that because they became figures in the scientific and engineering world.

Q: How did you find the adaptation to scholastic life in PG school after having been so active in combat?

Admiral Michaelis: I had a very difficult time, more than anything else, in the adjustment. I had two small children, and we had a terrible time finding places to live. I lived in four different places in Annapolis in a period of eight months.

Q: It wasn't only difficult for you; it must have been awfully difficult for your wife.

Admiral Michaelis: It was terrible. We finally got up to MIT, and things kind of got straightened out. It was up there that I had gotten far enough along that I said I really wasn't interested in busting out of this thing. So I settled down and went to work and found a great deal of interest in many of the things that I was doing.

Q: You must have had to parcel your time, however, and didn't have much family time.

Admiral Michaelis: No, not much family life. We were even working weekends.

---

* This is discussed in the Naval Institute oral history of Vice Admiral Edwin B. Hooper, USN (Ret.).

Q: You came out with a degree?

Admiral Michaelis: Yes, an M.S. in aeronautical engineering.

Q: Was there any attempt at supervision on the part of the Navy Department when you were a student there? Were there other Navy people in your group?

Admiral Michaelis: Yes, there was a group of seven of us. We had the misfortune to follow a group of 11 in which only two finished. Right at the end of the war, MIT was upgrading its academics. They had been through a great depression during the war. With the class just ahead of us, after the first six months MIT went back to the Navy and asked the Navy to remove several of them, which it did. They were not going to be able to make the academics as they had been operating during the course of that year. So that put a little pressure on us.

Anyway, the contacts between the Navy and the bureaus and the people who were the sponsors for the course were carried on mainly through a representative of the bureau up there at MIT. He was a Navy captain; we saw a bit of him, not very much. We had more contact with the Navy through what Draper was doing with the Navy than any effort to flow contact between the resident representative who sat between us and our sponsors.

Q: Did Draper have a specific project with the Navy under way at that point?

Admiral Michaelis: He had two or three. They were small, but they were tributary projects to missile systems, in the guidance area. He was building very fine integrated accelerometers and so forth at that time for inertial systems. He was one of the first ones in this country to set up a clean room. They kept the atmosphere perfectly clear of dust and all particles, so that these gyros that have a very, very low precession rate would not be upset.

I did a thesis by instrumenting a B-25 airplane at Hanscom Air Force Base; the results were mailed to the university.* I did some measurements in dynamics, investigating theory against actual measurements. It was more developing methods of measurements than anything else.

Q: Was that utilized in any way?

Admiral Michaelis: Yes, it was utilized, and it was made a part of the reference book system of MIT in the aero department. A couple of pretty good things came out of it--nothing that went on tablets of stone, but they were useful.

VX-3 was the next duty, and it was most interesting. I had an opportunity to use some of the attention I had given to projectizing--if I can use some Pentagonese--work in VX-3. We were in the transition stage at that point between conventional and jet aircraft. That was a tremendously interesting period.

Q: This was called Air Development Squadron Three. Where was it based?

Admiral Michaelis: Yes, it was, and it was based at Atlantic City, New Jersey. It just happened to be a field that was available. Atlantic City has always been one of those marginal fields--marginal from the viewpoint that next year it was going to be put out of commission, so very, very few improvements were made to it. Today it is the R&D field for FAA.†

Our effort in VX-3 was to develop tactics in the transition between conventional and jet aircraft and to develop them for shipboard use. So we would make maybe four deployments aboard ship every year for two to three weeks at a crack to work out the things we had developed ashore.

---

* Hanscom Field, as it was then known, was 18 miles northwest of Boston. The B-25 Mitchell was the type of bomber used for the Doolittle raid on Tokyo in April 1942.
† R&D--research and development; FAA--Federal Aviation Administration.

We developed tactics for defense, for strike, for all-weather approaches to the ship, for all-weather handling of multiple aircraft for all-weather approaches to the ship. And we were in fairly crude days. I recall when we practiced out let-downs in real weather to Atlantic City. We used to home onto the radio station at the end of the Steel Pier. That was our let-down point, out to sea, and back again to the field.

Q: You were known as the project coordinator. Did you dream up some of these projects, or were they supplied by the fleet?

Admiral Michaelis: Most of them came from the fleet, but we made extensive trips to the fleet and in many cases urged them to get these projects started, because we had equipment that they were going to get but that they didn't yet have. Although all of these projects were either coming from the Chief of Naval Operations in Washington or directly from the fleet, we were the catalysts with the fleet very often to get these projects started.

Q: You were, in fact, an aeronautical OpDevFor, weren't you?

Admiral Michaelis: Yes, Operational Development Force in those days rather than OpTEvFor, Operational Test and Evaluation Force, later on.[*]

Q: That was a kind of parallel operation--the fleet feeding in their needs to the development people on shore.

Admiral Michaelis: That's right, and what we were supposed to do was also to sit in the saddle position between the fleet and new equipment so that when people got new equipment they had some idea as starters as to how to use it tactically, not just what they read out of a handbook. Among the kinds of things we did were the first all-weather work for groups of aircraft; a lot of development of tactics; and we shot a considerable amount of

---

[*] The command was renamed in May 1959.

gunnery. With a jet airplane you had no better guns than you had in the conventional propeller airplanes, but you had to make a different kind of pass, because the airplanes flew somewhat differently. We made a flatter pass, as we used to say. We tried to establish the techniques for learning how to shoot the guns in the jet airplanes.

Q: Did your squadron act as a kind of cell unit when you developed equipment there in a tactical sense, and it was available to the fleet? Did you send someone from your squadron out to the fleet to demonstrate?

Admiral Michaelis: Most of the work was done through reports and then visits. The fleet was constantly calling for visits from VX-3 and VX-4. We made visits to the ships, but most of our work ended up in written reports and some movies. The Korean War was just beginning to build up at the time. We had an interesting thing; we had to do something about the trains in Korea.

Q: You certainly did--in the tunnels.

Admiral Michaelis: We established a project and got it approved in which we flew at low altitudes over a good portion of the railroads in the eastern part of the United States. We photographed, through gunsights, the built-up embankments. The idea was to be able to put the right kind of forward-firing charges, at very low altitude, into the sides of these embankments and cave in the railroad on top of the ties. It was one heck of a good theory, but we didn't have the right kinds of munitions to do it. We didn't had shaped charges in those days; we didn't have properly fuzed heavy munitions that you could lay into the side of a hill. We needed good, long-delay fuzes. We didn't use much in the way of long-delay fuzes in World War II, so we didn't have any developed when the Korean War came along.

Q: How did you operate in terms of live tests?

Admiral Michaelis: We didn't. We took those pictures, and then we went to Inyokern--China Lake, California--and had them construct some of these mock things. Then we went after them to find out what would happen. We didn't do very well on that, simply because we had the wrong munitions. It was a good idea, but we didn't have the equipment to exploit it.

Q: Was some variant on it actually put into operation?

Admiral Michaelis: It was, but, again, it didn't have the universal application we had hoped it was going to have. Every railroad has two or three things in common, and one of these things was that they had to build the track up at various places along the road. You don't go very many miles in a railroad that you don't have fills of some kind--someplace where you can get the airplane down almost as low as the track. You are flying slightly below the track at that particular point, and it gave you an excellent opportunity to lay in with great accuracy, with nobody around to bother you. The train may be down the track 100 miles or 50 miles or 25 miles, but you had a good opportunity to go in unopposed at low altitude without any special fire-control equipment. You could throw these things into the side of the hill by releasing them just before you are going to hit the hill, and you pop right up above the hill. Those of us who worked on it, and those who were monitoring it, felt it an excellent way. I give you this as an example.

Q: You didn't have the same number of tunnels, did you, that the Koreans have?

Admiral Michaelis: No, not at all.

Q: What tie-in did you have with industry itself when you were testing some of these things?

Admiral Michaelis: Very little. We had industry representatives, but from the viewpoint of making sure that the equipment was working properly. For example, when we got the first

OME--omnidirectional homing equipment--that gave both bearing and distance, a rep came on board to make sure of the equipment, to determine how reliable the equipment was. We always had reps from the various engine and aircraft companies aboard. Our instrumentation, since it was for fleet projects, was very, very simple. We had a few Brown recorders and things like that which were kept up by sailors, blue-suiters. We didn't have a great need for sizable association of industry at that point, and industry was only beginning to delve into some of these new areas. They were still living very much off the fat of World War II. Things that hadn't been finished in development in World War II were being worked on by industry for the following five years.

Q: And I suppose you were concerned about the surplus materials left over from World War II.

Admiral Michaelis: That is very much so.

Q: You were for ten months project manager, and then you became the exec for the whole outfit. What difference was there in your status or your responsibilities?

Admiral Michaelis: Going from a project coordinator to an exec is not a very pleasant move, going from a fairly exciting project to shuffling an awful lot of papers. Unfortunately, the exec of the squadron was killed.

Q: In one of the tests?

Admiral Michaelis: No. I was flying on his wing when he was killed. Something happened to him physically in the cockpit. I don't know--he either got an oxy or had a heart attack or something. He was a well-known Navy football player, Lemuel D. Cooke, out of the class of '39.[*]

---

[*] Lieutenant Commander Lemuel D. Cooke, USN, died in a plane crash at Atlantic City, New Jersey, on 17 May 1950.

My next duty was in the Naval Air Special Weapons Facility, and it didn't become that until after I had been there for about a year and a half. It was sort of an unusual introduction to a new job. I went to Albuquerque, which was the center for all nuclear development in the applications process, moving from the nuclear devices into actual weaponry and the tests of these air-dropped weapons off of aircraft.

The AEC target was the one that was right out in the middle of the Salton Sea.[*] We flew from Albuquerque to the Salton Sea to make these drops. Actually, the drops of shapes were under the aegis of the AEC, but they used military equipment. So there was a great deal of fallout in this thing for both the Air Force and the Navy in learning about the tactical end and the users' end of nuclear weapons. When I got out there, there was no Navy; it was all Air Force. My job was to do the first work.

Q: How did you happen to get selected for that?

Admiral Michaelis: Well, the man who proceeded me was Tom Walker, a friend of mine.[†] He was over in Sandia Base, which was the place where they developed and trained people to operate all the nuclear weapons, whether they were from the Army's howitzers, air-dropped weapons, or straight munitions. He simply called me up one day and told me what he was doing and asked me if I would be interested in coming there. They happened to be sort of in God's province in those days: whomever they wanted out there, they got. It was that important to the Navy to start moving into an area wherein they had been foreclosed because they couldn't carry the big weapons that the Air Force carried--the old O-6 and the Fat Man and so forth, the Mark 4 and 5. It wasn't until we got around to the Mark 5 weapon and then the Mark 7 and the Mark 8 that we got weapons that were tactically amenable to use aboard carrier aircraft.[‡]

---

[*] AEC--Atomic Energy Commission. The Salton Sea is in southeast California.
[†] Lieutenant Commander Thomas J. Walker III, USN.
[‡] For details and illustrations of these various weapons, see Chuck Hansen, U.S. Nuclear Weapons: The Secret History (New York: Orion Books [Crown Publishers, Inc.], 1988).

Q: Was the prevailing attitude in the Navy at that point that if a man got selected for this kind of thing that it was for the balance of his career--he wasn't going to get out of it again? Did you feel that?

Admiral Michaelis: I don't think there was ever anything written about that, but it certainly became usage at that particular point.

Q: That is something that Bob Wertheim told me.* I think he was out there at about the same time.

Admiral Michaelis: I struggled against that, because I figured that that was just part of what you had to do and something you needed to be conversant with in the Navy.

Anyway, at that particular time it was one of the most interesting jobs that any man ever had and one of the most frustrating. I was owned by nobody; I was in a facility that was attached to a detachment in Kirtland Air Force Base, what we called "across the tracks." When I reported in there, it was just comical; nobody knew where this naval air facility was, and that is what it was called at the time.

I finally found it, and when I got there I found no airplanes on the ramp. What passed for our hangar was the remains of an AJ which had crashed out off the Los Lunas bombing range, on which you made practice drops; the range was near Albuquerque. But you didn't drop any real shapes like they did out over the Salton Sea. Anyway, it was an interesting introduction to what my job was going to be. But very quickly I found I had no airplanes, and I had a lot to do and not much help in doing it.

The job was to take mainly the Mark 7 bomb, which was 30 inches in diameter and of different density than any weapons we had ever worked with before. It was a low-density weapon, and for its size it didn't have very much inertia around any of its axes. That meant it was going to be difficult to get it away from the airplane. It was so big, and the wings of the airplane were so close to the ground, that you had to push the thing right up

---

* Rear Admiral Robert H. Wertheim, USN (Ret.), is the subject of a Naval Institute oral history.

against the rear end. We ran into some interesting things to solve. I must say we got them solved, but not in the manner that I think the National Academy of Science would have thought was the best way to do them.

Q: These were in-house solutions?

Admiral Michaelis: Yes, and eventually refined under the AEC and accepted and qualified. There was one wild one in the Mark 7. It had a very strange tail, and it was triangular.[*] Most weapons had a 90-degree separation between their fins, but this one had 120 degrees. The lower fin was down, and the upper two stuck up under the wing. The lower fin was retractable. So you would take off with it retracted, and when you got airborne you would lower that fin, and then it was ready to go. This bomb was so close to the wing and was in the influence of the wing. It would keep flopping up and jamming its tail into the wing every time we released it. We had no such thing in those days as a powered rack--what they called a displacement rack--so we had to find another way to do it.

What we finally did was to take off the tail cone, flip the tail around 180 degrees, and put the two fins down. They were at enough angle that they didn't bother you on takeoff or landing. We took the folding fin and spring-loaded it and put it up next to the wing. It was on a lanyard, and when it had fallen 18 feet away from the airplane, the lanyard would pull, and the thing would spring out. What it allowed you to do was that when you let that bomb go under the airplane, it would crank around and had enough clearance with its tail. By the time it developed enough downward thrust, just from the body of the bomb, it had cleared the airplane, and down there 18 feet away the lanyard would pull. These were kind of Rube Goldberg-type things we had to do, because the airplanes we were using to drop bombs were not designed to drop that type of bomb.[†] We had to do all sort of things. The two airplanes we did this on were Banshees, the old F2H,

---

[*] For illustrations, see Chuck Hansen, U.S. Nuclear Weapons: The Secret History, page 133.
[†] Reuben L. "Rube" Goldberg (1883-1970) was a popular syndicated newspaper cartoonist best known for drawings of mechanical devices that used absurdly unnecessary complexity to achieve simple actions.

and the Spad, the AD.* The AD problems were fairly simple, because you could get enough clearance.

About the only first I ever had in my life in the Navy was doing the first idiot loops. When we had bad weather, we had no way to get enough clearance to drop the bomb in a dive and pull out and get clear of the bomb's blast unless we had a minimum of 18,000 feet of clear weather, and that's not good enough, of course. So both the Air Force and the Navy started off on a development at almost the same time, using a reference point very, very low to the ground, underneath the overcast. You would pull up at a pre-timed point and let the bomb go at a known G loading. You would arc it over and down to the target while you completed the Immelmann and disappeared.† It did give you the opportunity to do low-altitude bombing without the kinds of equipment that you needed to do it on instruments and know where the target was because of a predetermined entry point.

It was a funny thing. I couldn't get anybody interested in this. We took an old toss-bombing equipment and modified it. By the time I had made 170 idiot loops to throw this bomb at the target and then took the results to Washington, it was just one of those things that came at the right time, and they said, "This is exactly what we need." And then I couldn't keep the people away from the place. So we joined up then with China Lake, and they took it over, because it was not up to us to continue this development.

But there was never any end to things out there of great interest.

Q: Was Chick Hayward out there then?‡

Admiral Michaelis: Chick was in and out all the time. He was even earlier, when he had VC-5. He was much earlier--in fact, in the very early days, between '45 and '50.

---

* The McDonnell F2H Banshee was one of the Navy's early jet fighters that had first entered fleet squadrons in 1949. The Douglas AD Skyraider was a propeller-driven attack plane that entered the fleet in 1948.
† An Immelmann turn is one in which an airplane in flight first makes half a loop and then rolls over to make the second half.
‡ Captain John T. Hayard, USN. The oral history of Hayward, who retired as a vice admiral, is in the Naval Institute collection.

Q: Where did your family live?

Admiral Michaelis: Right there in Albuquerque.

Q: Were they happy in this situation?

Admiral Michaelis: They enjoyed it very much. Kirtland Air Force Base is right on the edge of Albuquerque. I wasn't more than ten minutes from my office.

Q: I understand some of the families out in the desert were not too happy there.

Admiral Michaelis: It is an interesting thing--adaptation to the desert. When I first got there, I thought it was the end of all eternity. I just couldn't believe anybody could elect to live in that part of the country. I arrived in a sandstorm, which is a very unpleasant thing, and I arrived without my family. It is 5,200 feet in the air. Unless you know how altitude and dry heat affect your body, you've got to learn a little bit about your intakes, particularly alcohol. But after I was there for about a year and very much enjoying what I was doing, I got so I felt very depressed when I got up and the weather wasn't so beautiful that I could see Mount Taylor 60 miles away. Today I like the area very much; my whole family enjoyed it. We missed the water, however.

By the time I left there, we were then a command, a field activity under the Bureau of Aeronautics.

Q: You had grown up at that point as a unit out there?

Admiral Michaelis: Yes, and there were some tremendously funny things that happened in the course of doing that.

Interview Number 3 with Admiral Frederick H. Michaelis, U.S. Navy (Retired)

Place: Naval Historical Center, Washington, D.C.

Date: Friday, 29 January 1982

Interviewer: John T. Mason, Jr.

Q: I'd like to begin with a continuation of your remarks, Admiral, on the Albuquerque assignment.

Admiral Michaelis: I may have said this, but I would like to make note of the shortfall when we went from strategic to tactical bombing and the plan for it in nuclear weapons. Because of escape requirements, we went down this road for quite a ways without any means of delivery unless we had visual conditions. As I recall, for a weapon of about Mark 7 size, we had to have in the dive-bombing run at least 17,000 feet, which didn't do much for the accuracy. It also said that there were going to be weeks and weeks of time when you could not deliver attacks, if you were called on to do it, because of weather conditions. That's a rather extreme demand on good weather.

Q: Yes.

Admiral Michaelis: Without having the proper avionics and so forth on that day, I think one of the most interesting tactical periods that I have known particularly was the development of the lofting system.

To begin with, it was called loft bombing; it came to be called toss bombing later. This was a means where you would come in under the overcast and pick up a visual starting point for timing a run, and then pulling up on a programmed G rate, acceleration rate. Your bomb was automatically released when you were up at 45 or 50 or whatever the proper combination of angles for distance to the target. The bomb would release and you would proceed on instruments to complete an Immelmann. The bomb would proceed on its way, and you would proceed in the opposite direction as you came out.

I think this was one of the anomalies of air warfare--the loft-bombing technique--because it was something that there wasn't a necessity for, that nobody would really think of doing. After training people to do an Immelmann on instruments, it seemed strange that you would release a weapon during the course of it. But it was a very successful tactic, and we were stuck with it for many, many years.

Q: It simply evolved.

Admiral Michaelis: Yes, yes. It was something that was needed. We neither had the type of weapons that you could lay on the ground and fly away from them and some moment later they would go off. We didn't have that kind of delay system in order to adapt to delivery of weapons in weather. This was about the best thing we could devise, and we started all that out at Albuquerque. The Air Force and the Navy worked on this together. People look back on this in history and will understand that this thing was born of necessity. In almost everything we did when we were moving from the strategic to the tactical area of bombing, we were doing all sorts of new things.

First of all, we were putting bombs on aircraft that were never designed to carry them. So we had to do all sorts of makeshift types of things. Strangely enough, because it was needed to complete the delivery requirement, the AEC approved the things. I'm sure that would make them shudder right now. But I did want to add that, because you don't do that much in the way of loft bombing these days, practicing for it and so forth. The weapons are different, and they can be laid down and so forth so that you don't have to go through this. But it was sort of an anomaly in the sequence of tactical development, and I thought it was fairly interesting.

That was an interesting complex at Albuquerque. You know, it was really divided into two parts. The field command, AFSWP, was armed forces special weapons and was at

Sandia Base.* The Special Weapons Center of the Air Force and the Naval Air Special Weapons Center were over at Kirtland Air Force Base. It was a pretty high level of activity in those days: a lot going on, a lot of new ground being broken. It was sort of exciting making the first tactical bomb drops at supersonic speeds and understanding what the separation was going to do without having much foreknowledge of how it was going to go, whether there would be floaters or not and so forth.

Q: It's fun being a pioneer.

Admiral Michaelis: Oh, it was magnificent. Nobody really knew what to do next, and if they did know, they were so far away that we usually had it done before they told us to go do it.

Q: Well, you told me last time that your family was very happy out there, that they liked the desert.

Admiral Michaelis: Yes, they did.

Q: So you must have been reluctant to leave.

Admiral Michaelis: I was reluctant. There was a lot going on, and I had very close ties with China Lake and with the AEC target complex out of the Salton Sea.

Q: What was China Lake doing at that point?

Admiral Michaelis: Once we had developed this business of loft bombing, we had to jury-rig a release system. Then we dropped about 150 practice bombs and plotted them all and took them to Washington. All the time we were trying to get somebody's attention.

---

* AFSWP--Armed Forces Special Weapons Project.

Then, when we got their attention, it was overwhelming. It was a better mousetrap, so we headed that off to China Lake and went on with our basic business of developing the capability to drop tactical nuclear weapons. It was sort of the last I had to do with nuclear weapons except as an active pilot. In other words, unlike a lot of people, I didn't stay with nuclear weapons.

Q: As we mentioned last time, this was a pattern--that a man stayed with in once he got introduced to it.

Admiral Michaelis: Very much so. Generally that was so.

Q: How did you break loose?

Admiral Michaelis: I did so consciously. I just plain didn't want to get stuck in the nuclear weapon environment. Well, I take it back. I had that tour with the JSTPS later on.[*] I just really felt like there was so much need to tie tactical nuclear capability to conventional capability and make sure you knew where the crossover points took place. We had to be prepared in our carrier task groups--what are now battle groups--in the handling of both conventional and nuclear weapons within the confines of a carrier.

Q: You certainly weren't taken in, then, by the idea of massive retaliation--all eggs in one basket in terms of turning one's back on the conventional and concentrating on the nuclear.[†]

Admiral Michaelis: We came very close to making that terrible mistake along that line.

---

[*] JSTPS--Joint Strategic Target Planning Staff, which is discussed in the Naval Institute oral histories of several officers who were assigned there: Admiral John J. Hyland, USN (Ret.); Vice Admiral Gerald E. Miller, USN (Ret.); Vice Admiral Kent L. Lee, USN (Ret.); Vice Admiral Edward N. Parker, USN (Ret.).

[†] The massive retaliation strategy was articulated during the administration of President Dwight Eisenhower (1953-57). No nuclear weapons were employed under that strategy.

Q: But your whole idea was contrary to that. You bridged the two.

Admiral Michaelis: I wanted to make sure that whatever we were called on, whatever alternatives were necessary to exercise the flexibility that we should have as sea forces, that we were able to do it, and it's a tough business. You have to dedicate a certain amount of your ship to this, a certain amount of your ship to that, and a certain amount of your capabilities in aircraft to this and a certain amount of capabilities to that. Then you've got to crowd them all on one ship, and you have to do a lot of different things. It's always been a very prominent problem, I think, to be constantly looked after in carrier aviation.

Q: Well, shall we go on now to the Kearsarge in 1954?[*]

Admiral Michaelis: Yes. The Korean War was over, and we were involved in the evacuation of the Tachen Islands.[†] A sort of low stability point in the Pacific followed that period. It was not an overwhelmingly exciting tour as air group commander.[‡] I would have liked it much better to have it be a little earlier. So that went on a little over a year. I guess the main thing that went on in that period was an effort to try to change the composition of the air group. I went out with a different air group in composition than any of the rest of them at that time. We had a heavier all-weather capability than was the one in the past. Instead having four all-weather Banshee-3's, we went out with eight all-weather Banshee-3s.

---

[*] The USS Kearsarge (CVA-33) was first commissioned 2 March 1946, later recommissioned 15 February 1952 after a modernization period. She had a standard displacement of 38,000 tons, was 888 feet long, 129 feet in the beam, and had an extreme width of 147 feet. Her top speed was 33 knots. She had eight 5-inch guns, 28 3-inch guns, and could accommodate approximately 80 aircraft.

[†] The small Tachen Islands, north of Formosa (as Taiwan was then called) were subject to attack from mainland China in the early 1950s. From 6 to 13 February 1955, on the advice of the U.S. Government and with the assistance of the U.S. Seventh Fleet, the Nationalist Chinese evacuated 18,000 civilians and 20,000 military personnel from the Tachens.

[‡] Commander Michaelis was commander Carrier Air Group 11.

Q: Was this something of your design?

Admiral Michaelis: Oh, absolutely, yes. I just was convinced that as far as an all-weather, all-around capability, we were shortsighted in regard to weather. I don't know that we did all that well in proving that this was a desirable thing. It so often happens when you press a point, which you say, "I want to change my organization," by the time people finally get around to doing it, you don't have much time to train. So I took out a pretty green all-weather squadron, which I was putting all my hopes on as to giving us a better balance in the air group.

Q: Did you have much of a struggle to achieve that, to get permission to do that?

Admiral Michaelis: Yes. The Navy's institutionalized around sort of what they've got, and most times they work very hard to get it, both in terms of acquiring and in learning how to use it. Changes don't come easily.

Q: Unless you're persuasive.

Admiral Michaelis: Unless you're persistent.

Q: Whom did you have to convince for this?

Admiral Michaelis: Well, I had to convince the air type commander on the West Coast, and I had to convince the people in Washington.* Then there really wasn't much of a job. If he thought he could do it, if he thought it was worthwhile, he didn't have much trouble convincing people--as long as you didn't ask them for a lot of money or a lot of resources. Do it within what you've got. That's the age-old way of getting something--do it out of your socks.

---

* The type commander was Commander Air Force Pacific Fleet (ComAirPac).

Q: And you say the results were not completely to your satisfaction?

Admiral Michaelis: They weren't, because there was really no way of proving that we had gotten there yet. But I will say we were right on the edge then of an extensive upgrade in all kinds of aircraft in ability to handle weather and mostly on the terminal end. That's coming back or getting off of the carriers, and not as much on the target end. That came even later and is still coming.

Q: Well, this involved new types of airplanes.

Admiral Michaelis: They were the early days. It was the third operational model of the McDonnell series: the F1H, the F2H, and the F2H-3. It was the 3s that were all weather, you know, in name--not honestly, but better than before.

Q: This involved some consultation, did it not, with the manufacturers, too, and designers?

Admiral Michaelis: Yes, and in those days we worked a lot more closely with aerodynamicists and so forth and grew up with the airplane much more than we do today at the flying level, at the operational level.

Q: Why would you say that's true?

Admiral Michaelis: I think that we were not as well prepared then as we are now. We're pretty careful now. If we have a new airplane, a new set of tactics for a given airplane, or new pieces in the airplane, I think we're pretty careful to prepare the people who are going to operate them. Before they ever get to sea, before they ever get out on a carrier, they have to know that equipment. At the most, it's necessary to learn how to use it at sea. You go to sea knowing how to use it. I have to say in those earlier days, first of all, we didn't have a lot of sophisticated equipment. They were just on margin at that particular point with the advent of jet airplanes: We didn't have the infrastructure ashore to fill in that gap that the readiness squadrons--they call them replacement air groups now--provide today. This is really quite advanced training for new equipment you're going to be using, and it's an absolute necessity today, because with so many airplanes like the A-6 and so forth, you just have to train an assistant, or you're not going to be able to operate under operational conditions.*

Q: That's very interesting, because it reflects something I heard this morning on the SSBN project.† There is training in advance so that when a unit is sent out to Canaveral or someplace like that, they're set to go. They train to the point where they don't have to flub around.

Admiral Michaelis: I know that's true; that certainly is true. They have the best continuity of training of any of the forces in the Navy.

Q: Yes. But what you're saying seems to imply the same thing in terms of air.

Admiral Michaelis: If you were to rank the various forces in terms of degree of training and, therefore, readiness, you would naturally assume that those forces that had to do with the survivability--that are vital to the United States--are going to have the greatest level of training. And that's the SSBNs; they are an extremely important part of the triad, and that means that you are going to whatever extreme is necessary to make sure that they are training and not consider it an extreme.‡ That's the case. It's the case with SAC, it's the case with our SSBNs, and I would say then the next little niche coming down on that training is aviation.§ And it's particularly true for carrier aviation, simply because it's a very,

---

* The Grumman A-6 Intruder attack plane has a side-by-side cockpit with the pilot on the left and the bombardier-navigator on the right.
† SSBN--nuclear-powered ballistic missile submarine.
‡ The "triad" of U.S. nuclear weapons delivery vehicles consists of submarines, land-based missiles, and manned bombers.
§ SAC--Strategic Air Command.

very specialized type of aviation, first of all. Only two or three navies have carriers, which are necessary for worldwide operation if you intend to go in harm's way. Therefore, it's expensive. The equipment you operate is expensive, and you'd better learn to make the most out of what you've got so you can do it well.

I think the training is very good. As a matter of fact, it's getting harder and harder with people up through the level of lieutenant commander to get them to do anything except stay right with what they're trying to learn to do in aviation. We just don't send very many of the pilots to postgraduate school and the war colleges. They come off a squadron, and the best ones are sent to the RAG to train the next people coming along. I'm deviating.

Q: That's interesting and an important deviation. Then doesn't this lead eventually to some rearrangement of the traditional Navy promotion system, if a man is staying with a job?

Admiral Michaelis: Well, I think in the last ten years there have been some modifications to the promotional system which have taken cognizance of the fact that there is so much to do in certain specialized areas that you can't train everybody to be the CNO these days. It just can't be done.

There is still a great deal of hewing to the line of patterned careers, but at the same time it's not as patterned as it used to be. We're going to see more and more of this moving away from the pattern, I think, in the future. The more sophisticated things get, the more time you require.

Q: The more necessary.

Admiral Michaelis: Yes. Well, let's see. That sort of closes out the air group. It was not a highly eventful tour of duty.

Q: Well, it didn't compare to combat that you were engaged on in the Randolph or anything like that.

Admiral Michaelis: Let me say something about that time. Those were the darkest days of carrier aviation. We were trying to adapt underpowered jets to straight-deck carriers. We were having a considerable amount of trouble with a plane that didn't catch a wire, not being properly arrested by the holding gear and ending up in the pack forward and cleaning out three or four or five or six airplanes. It was a ruinous time. So they kept putting that barricade higher and higher, those big nylon barricades, and they finally got them up to 32 feet. So you had to commit yourself way out to what you were going to do. I will mention that as sort of a turning point, just after I had my shot at being an air group commander.

Fortunately, there were three things that came along, and you've heard this from other people. All of them came from the Brits, and they saved carrier aviation, just plain saved it. If somebody were to say today, you know, what's the biggest influence on carrier aviation with the advent of jets, I would say the British Navy.

Q: And how unfortunate. They don't have very much in that area now.

Admiral Michaelis: They had a wonderful place there at Bedford, you know, the Naval Experimental--they did all kinds of things out there. They developed the angled deck; they developed the mirror landing system; the steam catapult, and so forth.

Q: And those came along sort of cluster-like?

Admiral Michaelis: Yes, they did. They really sort of clustered together.

Q: Were they the result of their World War II experiences?

Admiral Michaelis: I would say that they were the result of just the basically fine capability of the Brits to prototype but not produce. I think it's an honestly stated characteristic of the Brits. They had been working ever since World War II to do something about those horrible hydraulic catapults, and, of course, the steam catapult was a dream alongside those hydraulics. But I was sort of at the bitter end. I mean, I had an air group right at the bitter end, and we fought every day to make sure that our safety record was preserved. Nowadays, nobody ever looks at a dash pot on a tailhook other than for periodic inspections. We used to check those dash pots every single day. We had a lot more wires then, but you also had a much greater need to catch them, to hook them.

Q: Was there much publicity given to accidents in that time? I simply can't recall.

Admiral Michaelis: Yes, there was.

Q: The kind of publicity they give now if something happens on the Nimitz?[*]

Admiral Michaelis: No, because we were still under the influence of the high loss rates of World War II and the Korean War. We were so fresh from the Korean War that people inside knew the accident rate was high, and they heard a lot about it. As a matter of fact, the people who were providing dollars for the Navy--some people in OSD, people in Congress--were beginning to question whether aviation had an acceptable role flying off the carriers.[†]

Q: After the experience of World War II?

Admiral Michaelis: It was just that . . .

Q: Sense of frustration.

---

[*] On the night of 26 May 1981, several months before this interview, a Marine Corps EA-6B electronic warfare plane crashed on the flight deck of the aircraft carrier Nimitz (CVN-68) while attempting to land.
[†] OSD--Office of the Secretary of Defense.

Admiral Michaelis: We were beginning to run out of airplanes that we had stashed away in the desert, and, really, if we were going to stay up front in the war at sea, we really had to take jets to sea. But they were a different breed of cat. You know, those early power plants were terrible. Some of them were very reliable, but so far as having enough thrust at low speed, they were terrible.

There was a lot of good that came to carrier aviation in the jet airplanes, though. At a very high speed, strength that had to be built in the airplanes reduced the delta between the land-based airplane and carrier-based airplane. It was necessary to put in the keel strength and the landing gear strength and so forth to take arrestments in catapults. The density of the planes became very high, the strength requirements just to take care of the aerodynamic loads in supersonic, transonic, subsonic flight was so much greater. The difference between the weight of a carrier-based and a land-based aircraft began to diminish so it was a big plus there. Wing fold was about the only thing you had to pay for, a side remark.

After that, a little short tour.

Q: Again in special weapons.

Admiral Michaelis: Special weapons at AirPac.

Q: Who was AirPac?

Admiral Michaelis: At the time it was Beauty Martin.[*]

Q: How did you justify your title, special weapons officer?

---

[*] Vice Admiral Harold M. Martin, USN, served as Commander Air Force Pacific Fleet from 1 April 1952 to 1 February 1956.

Admiral Michaelis: Well, we provided the training syllabi, and we went out and inspected. We were just getting into special weapons spaces in a carrier. We were always--and we do to this day--we talked about the capability of carrying nuclear weapons; we never talk about carrying them.

Q: Well, I suppose there's some psychological reason.

Admiral Michaelis: Oh, yes, there is. When you go into somebody's harbor, you never say when you've got them aboard or not. And, incidentally, that little subterfuge has been going on for 30 years, maybe longer.

There was one very interesting thing that went on during that time. The hydrogen bomb was making its entry into carriers, and there was a great demand for greater assurance, simply because of the frightening strength relative to previous weapons that was available with a hydrogen bomb. Eisenhower decided that we had to have a civilian representative from AEC to carry the keys for the ship.[*]

Q: Always?

Admiral Michaelis: I think one of the worst jobs I ever had in my life was to go around to these COs of the carriers and the cardiv commanders and say, "The good news is you're going to get these Mark 15 weapons aboard, and the bad news is you've got a babysitter."[†] You just can't imagine the reaction.

Q: I can imagine, yes. But they had to comply.

---

[*] Dwight D. Eisenhower was President of the United States from 1953 to 1961.
[†] COs--commanding officers; cardiv--carrier division. For details on the Mark 15, see Chuck Hansen, U.S. Nuclear Weapons: The Secret History, pages 145-146.

Admiral Michaelis: There was nothing else they could do, and I really can remember I took some brutal abuse, as though I owned those birds and this was my decision. That's the only thing I can remember during that period.

Q: Let me ask about these poor fellows from the AEC. How did they cope with boredom?

Admiral Michaelis: Well, they became the best acey-deucy players in the wardroom, and, fortunately, it didn't last very long.* It lasted about a year and a half, and then they got to the place where they had sufficient confidence in the system which required more than one authority--the two-man rule and so forth was pretty well established, and safeguards were myriad.

I can remember Martin called me in and told me that I was to get myself well versed in this thing, and I could go around and inform the commanding officers. I said, "You'd be well advised, if I may say so, to go tell them yourself." They wouldn't talk back so readily. But he was just as embarrassed about it as everybody else was, so he sent Michaelis.

Q: I suppose the President simultaneously was struggling with the overall security business.

Admiral Michaelis: Oh, he was. And he had detractors that were in very strong positions. But within about a couple of years, they would begin to realize that so far as security was concerned, the best place to have a nuclear capability was aboard ships, because their ability to contain and safeguard and so forth was much higher aboard a ship that it was from a land-based depot.

Q: When you say "they," you don't include the Air Force, however.

Admiral Michaelis: No, I don't include them, not at all. I'll just say one other thing about nuclear weapons. Down the road in the Navy was the only activity that didn't have to have

---

* Acey-deucy is a nautical version of the board game backgammon.

the PAL--personal lockout devices. In addition to all the fuzing and so forth were disabling devices that required very, very special people to come, and they're sort of the keepers of the weapon and turn the key in them. But it was very fortunate, I think, because by the time they came along and the necessity for them was born in people's minds, this had to do more with a multinational utilization of the weapons--our NATO allies and so forth. The Navy didn't have to go through that.

Well, that was a sort of uneventful thing. Then I was pulled out of there in the middle of the winter, I recall very clearly, by a captain named Tom Moorer, who had just become executive assistant to the Assistant Secretary of the Navy for Air.[*] He very unceremoniously pulled me up to Washington to be in that office. That was my first tour of duty in Washington.

Q: And Moorer was responsible for this?

Admiral Michaelis: Moorer was responsible for it. I had gotten to known Moorer when he was out at China Lake when I was in Albuquerque. Let's see if there was anything worthwhile there.

Q: The Assistant Secretary for Air was Smith, was it?

Admiral Michaelis: Jim Smith and then Garrison Norton.[†] My tour was more with Garrison Norton than Jim Smith. I guess I had maybe four or five or six months with Jim Smith, and he was a very capable man--very cold, though. Garrison Norton was just a warm, down-to-earth guy but was so smart about things. He recognized that the Assistant Secretary for Air couldn't expect to accomplish a lot, so he set his hand on things that were

---

[*] Captain Thomas H. Moorer, USN. Later, as an admiral, Moorer served as Chief of Naval Operations, 1967-70, and Chairman of the Joint Chiefs of Staff, 1970-74.
[†] James Hopkins Smith held the position from 23 July 1953 to 20 June 1956 and Garrison R. Norton from 28 June 1956 to 5 February 1959.

important that he could do. Along with Red Raborn, he had a lot to do with getting the Navy out of the Jupiter and into the Polaris.*

Q: That was quite an accomplishment.

Admiral Michaelis: You bet it was. I can remember that day down at Huntsville, Alabama, when I was carrying bags and so forth, when the Navy dropped the bomb on the Air Force at that meeting. The Navy's position was that with the new weapons available it couldn't abide to take that Jupiter capability in terms of range or in terms of additional bang. We had to take it in reduced size of warhead and must contain it in a weapon that would go as far as solid propellant would take it.†

Q: Now, that was about November 1956, was it not?

Admiral Michaelis: I'm sorry; I don't know the date. But, yes, I'm sure that was the time. That was a historical meeting.

Q: Tell me in more detail about it.

Admiral Michaelis: Well, von Braun and the Army commander, Medaris.‡ And, you know, I saw Medaris maybe 20 years later, and he's a churchman. He renovated an Episcopal church.

---

* Rear Admiral William F. Raborn, USN, was director of the Special Projects Office, which developed the fleet ballistic missile system. He held the post from 1955 to 1962, being promoted to vice admiral in 1960. His Polaris oral history is in the Naval Institute collection.
† The Jupiter was a liquid-fuel rocket, considered more dangerous for shipboard use than solid fuel.
‡ Wernher von Braun was a German-born rocket scientist who helped develop rockets for his country in World War II, then emigrated to the United States in 1945. He subsequently played a considerable role in the U.S. space program. Brigadier General John B. Medaris, USA, was Chief of Army Ordnance.

Q: Is he a priest in the church?

Admiral Michaelis: Yes. I reminded him of that meeting, and I thought he was going to burst into tears. He said that was one of the worst days of his life. He said, "I really couldn't understand how the Navy could do that." It was more of a surprise than I think anybody in our office thought it was going to be. They also thought, you know, that the Navy would never get the funding to go it alone. But the Navy did, and Garrison Norton was a tower of strength in that period. He didn't do very much else, and that was good too.

Q: Burke must have had a hand in that.*

Admiral Michaelis: You bet he did. It was a terribly difficult period for Burke, though. He didn't want to give up that air-breathing missile that he had.† But as Burke stated it, "Look, we can get a ballistic missile, and we can't get the air breather. We'll go for what we can get, because the country's got to have one or the other--preferably both, but the country's got to have something." He foresaw the vulnerability of missiles ashore. Well, that's about the only thing I can think of that is just of passing historical interest there, that decision to go to Polaris.

A very dynamic guy was Red Raborn in those days and other days. He was a fine leader and had a gunner named Levering Smith that was with him that turned out to be a pretty reasonable scientist.‡

Q: Yes, indeed. How did you like being an aide?

---

* Admiral Arleigh A. Burke, USN, served as Chief of Naval Operations from 17 August 1955 to 1 August 1961. The oral history of his experiences in connection with the Polaris program is in the Naval Institute collection.
† This was the Regulus cruise-missile program. Burke chose to sacrifice it in order to use the funds for Polaris instead.
‡ Captain Levering Smith, USN, who was technical director of the Special Projects office that oversaw the development of Polaris.

Admiral Michaelis: I wasn't an aide, but everybody sort of took their turn at aiding. Garrison Norton had a Marine captain as his aide. He was a nephew of a very wonderful Navy test pilot who, during the war, singlehandedly when they were in a big hurry to get the F8F going, he tested that and followed on to the F6F.

Q: Trapnell?

Admiral Michaelis: Trapnell, yes; you are very good at these.[*] Trapnell's nephew was named Nick Trapnell, and he was the aide to the assistant secretary and everybody.[†] It was a very small office. There was no R&D at the time, so Air had the R&D job, and they had a special assistant for aviation, which I was, and a special assistant for R&D, which was another commander. I didn't really think that was the greatest job in the world, you know. Fortunately, I was associated with some very fine people, and I learned to write speeches.

Q: That's a useful asset.

Admiral Michaelis: Yes, very useful. Garrison Norton, not doing any of that or not having a feel for it, was so appreciative that people would do things for him.

Q: What was his background? I don't know about his background.

Admiral Michaelis: Well, I don't think he ever stayed very long at anything. He was a man with a great deal of wealth, and he enjoyed being the Assistant Secretary for Air, because he was an aficionado of aviation, and he had been in a consultant role in the missile business. In the early days of aviation Garrison Norton had an airplane that he had an extra fuel tank put in, and he did a lot of polar or near-polar type of flying in the northern part of Alaska. He flew the ice and looked for passages for ships. He was a man who had the wherewithal

---

[*] Captain Frederick M. Trapnell, USN.
[†] Captain Nicholas M. Trapnell, Jr., USMC.

Frederick H. Michaelis #3 - 74

to do whatever he wanted, and in between times he worked at interesting things. I never did know where he got his political clout as Secretary, but I think it had to do more with . . .

Q: Was he from the West Coast?

Admiral Michaelis: No, he was New England--New York, Boston. He lives here now.
    Next one was as exec of the Randolph.

Q: Yes, going back to your old ship.

Admiral Michaelis: Yes, second go-around in the Randolph. Those were the days when they were pushing COs through ships pretty fast. I got aboard with one and had him for two months and had another one for about 10 or 11 months, and had another one for two or three months.

Q: Was that in order to expedite experience or what?

Admiral Michaelis: Yes, that was it mainly, to build experience in a great number of people, and it has since been judged to be a mistake. I agree with that.

Q: Did you find the Randolph changed in any sense? Had some of these new innovations been introduced to her?

Admiral Michaelis: It was angled up. By that, it had been modified to a 27 Charlie configuration.* So it had sponsons to create a little more room, but there was nowhere near

---

* Under project 27C, carriers of the Essex (CVA-9) class received a number of modifications during the 1950s. Included were angled landing decks, improved primary flight control stations, new elevators, and enclosed hurricane bows. See U.S. Naval Institute Proceedings, September 1975, pages 58-69.

enough room to take care of the ship's crew and the air group's crew as it became more and more jet. It was a very, very crowded ship. As the hotel keeper, being the exec, I found that a great deal of the day-to-day problems had to do with living on a ship that was too crowded.

Q: There is hardly any solution for that.

Admiral Michaelis: No, just fight hard to keep it clean, find places where you could set up exercise rooms, and it would be a little bit of a break. Interesting days in the Mediterranean in those times. People who operated in the Mediterranean were housekeepers. There were several places you could go in the Mediterranean, and wherever you went, you carried your house on your back. You set up your shore patrol, and everything was done from the instant you moved into the port until the time you left.

In the Pacific there were only three or four places where you went, and they had sort of a fixed shore detachment, which was a tour of duty for the people who took care of the shore patrol. This simply came from the Korean War and having had so much activity in these limited waters out in the Pacific. The ports were always crowded, and therefore they had to have more structure to them and a little more rigorous policing of the environment when you went ashore.

In the Med it was all a lot of fun. You moved into someplace in Greece or France--wherever it might be--and you set up your own. You also made your contact with the local gendarmerie to try to make sure you had an understanding and to keep the boys out of the local slammer and get every man back to the ship. Those were all the duties.

Q: Politically, the Med was an exciting place, too, wasn't it?

Admiral Michaelis: Oh, yes, it was. The days of a great deal of transition and the days of Cat Brown, Sixth Fleet commander at the time.[*]

---

[*] Vice Admiral Charles R. Brown, USN, commanded the Sixth Fleet from August 1956 to September 1958.

My first skipper was Dog Smith, who was one of those few wonderful characters.*

Q: What's his first name?

Admiral Michaelis: Daniel Fletcher Smith--wonderful man. He ended up making flag, and his last duty was Chief of Information for the Navy. People really predicted that he wouldn't live very long after he retired, and he didn't.†

Then Lou Kirn was CO of the ship.‡ These were all people just tremendously different from each other, and all of them were very fine people in their own right. Lou Kirn was a football player at the Naval Academy and a halfback. Then he was the fellow that got over polio when he could only move one toe. He was really still getting over that when he was aboard the ship. He had a hard time getting around, but he did.

The last one was Smoke Strean, who later on, in Enterprise, was my flag commander when we went around the world.§

Q: Oh, did you go around with Smoke?

Admiral Michaelis: Yes. So my first experience with Smoke was with the Randolph. I got him through his first month, and I left the ship.

Q: That must have put an extra strain on you as the exec to have all these different regimes come on board.

Admiral Michaelis: I just assumed it was part of the scheme of things.

---

* Captain Daniel F. Smith, Jr., USN, commanded the USS Randolph (CVA-15) from August 1956 to August 1957.
† Admiral Smith retired in 1970 and died on 5 October 1971.
‡ Captain Louis J. Kirn, USN, commanded the Randolph from August 1957 to June 1958.
§ Captain Bernard M. Strean, USN, commanded the Randolph from June 1958 to March 1959. The oral history of Strean, who retired as a vice admiral, is in the Naval Institute collection.

Q: I think your philosophical bent must have served you in good stead many times.

Admiral Michaelis: Well, it was exciting. Even being the exec was exciting. I think anything with carrier life was exciting, almost any facet of it.

Q: The Med by that time was our lake, wasn't it? The Royal Navy had moved out.

Admiral Michaelis: Yes, moved out, and the U.S. Navy was there. We were fixed always at two carriers. NATO had gotten into its division that it carries to this day--two flanks and the center.* It's become much more flexible in later years, but in those days it wasn't.

One of the things in those days that I remember so clearly: the Navy was really very fastidious about not getting in a position where they were politically locked to any country. All of the fuel, all of the food, all of the stores came out of the United States. You had the vendors aboard to sell you the little accordions in Italy and so forth. But so far as our consumables aboard ship, they really, truly, and honestly came from the United States.

Q: And you didn't actually have a home port, did you, in the Med?

Admiral Michaelis: No, no, there was no home port. There was later on, a bit after that. They started home-porting some oilers, and then they started using oil from refineries in the Med. But that was a matter of necessity. When the Sixth Fleet was set up after World War II, there just was none of that in the recovery period of the Western European countries. They just didn't have the wherewithal to supply this, and so it was a matter of necessity. But we made the greatest political trade out of it, you know, by staying with the advertising that we were totally independent of the political influences of any of the countries along the littoral of the Mediterranean.

---

* These divisions were the northern flank around the Baltic and North Sea; southern flank on the Mediterranean; and central front in France and Germany.

Q: You still had access to some of the North African ports, didn't you?

Admiral Michaelis: Not very many at that time. We may have before or after, but we didn't have them. You could go to Morocco, but carriers didn't usually go to Morocco. You could go to Lebanon. We didn't go to Alexandria; we didn't go anywhere in Egypt at the time.

The biggest problem was continuity of training in the Med. We really didn't have many target facilities, training ranges, and so forth. One, the condition of the countries around the Med and, two, the crowded conditions proscribing an area that would be a range area. So it was very inadequate, and it always has been.

Q: Were the Russians at all evident in the Med at that time?

Admiral Michaelis: No, really sort of on both sides. They had been, and they later became--it was pretty quiet so far as the Soviets were concerned during that particular period. It heated up just about the time I left because of Lebanon, you know. I left about a month before the landings in Lebanon.[*] That took place when I was at the war college, which I never got through, so that was a lost weekend. I don't have anything in my record to show that I had ever been at the war college.

Q: Oh, really? How did you get to go there then?

Admiral Michaelis: I went with perfectly good credentials and so forth, but halfway through I was selected to be the alternate skipper of the Enterprise. I had to get out of there real quick and go to a deep-draft ship command. Then I could be qualified to start my

---

[*] On 15 July 1958, at the request of Lebanese President Camille Chamoun, two U.S. Marine battalion landing teams went ashore at Beirut. Their mission was to support the government of President Chamoun, who was threatened by both civil war and the prospect of foreign intervention.

training in the Rickover charm school and then be available in case Vince de Poix, who was the first skipper, broke a leg or something of this nature.*

Q: So you had to go to the oiler?

Admiral Michaelis: Went to the oiler, yes. I stopped the war college in mid-year.

Q: Was there anything interesting developing for you there at the war college?

Admiral Michaelis: Not really, but it was a wonderful experience for me. A lot of people have wondered whether the war college is worth its salt, but it was so good for me. I had never, never had the opportunity to listen to a whole series of people come in that were either expert in certain fields, or very articulate, or in many cases both--and attempt to change our way of thinking and really, really challenge us. Some of that used to make me so mad, because when I went there I was so parochial I was almost hopeless. I at least came out of there knowing how parochial I was. I got the better of the two semesters, the way they broke it down in those days. So for the period I was there, I thoroughly enjoyed it. I thought it was a perfect time for me to go someplace like that. There couldn't have been a better time.

Q: You mean career-wise?

Admiral Michaelis: No, I mean from giving me a better understanding of the world around me, the bigger picture to move that Navy into.

Q: I suppose that was part of the whole design of the war college.

---

* Vice Admiral Hyman G. Rickover, USN, ran the Navy's nuclear power program. Captain Vincent P. de Poix, USN, was the commanding officer when the aircraft carrier Enterprise (CVAN-65) was commissioned 25 November 1961.

Admiral Michaelis: It is. But there are a lot of people who say it's not very important; I say it is extremely important. It may not be for everybody, but it was for me.

Q: Well, I suppose so, because there are a lot of people, as you and I know, who were not very conscious of world affairs or very interested in them and parochial in terms of their vision.

Admiral Michaelis: I was so anxious, you know, to have my son in the war college. He's between steaming around on ships, you know, for 10 or 11 years with hardly a break. He knows ships well, and he knows what he's supposed to be doing, but he doesn't know anything about anything else around the world.

So it was a good half-tour, but, really, I don't think the war college--other than the vistas that it opened to you--was as well organized as it was later on.

Q: You think Turner added something?

Admiral Michaelis: No, I really can't say about what Turner gave to it.[*]

I think the war college has seen better times, but that is just my personal opinion with regard to that. It had a good activities dean, or whatever he was called at that time. He really got some fine people to come in and talk to us, just great.

Well, let me get on from that, because there really wasn't much there. Then I went to an oiler.

Q: What did you learn from the deep draft?

Admiral Michaelis: It was a great experience. See, I was not a captain; I was a commander at the time. Most people are captains when they go to their deep draft. It doesn't make any difference, except that I didn't expect to have to be thinking about this for a while, if ever.

---

[*] Vice Admiral Stansfield Turner, USN, served as president of the Naval War College from 30 June 1972 to 9 August 1974.

Make-you-learn for aviators is very, very good, you know. Aviators work harder at their deep draft than people who are used to port and starboarding around. They have a lot more to learn, and I think they become good ship handlers, because they understand relative motion and so forth. You've heard this said before, but I think it's a fact. I really worked very hard.

Q: I suppose you feel you're on your mettle, too; I mean, you're challenged.

Admiral Michaelis: I was going to go to an ammunition ship, Paricutin. By the time I got to the West Coast, the commodore of the service force got ahold of me and was telling me how much more I would get if I went to an oiler, and I knew there was something afoot. I got my orders changed to an oiler. I went to an oiler, the Tolovana, whose preceding commanding officer had just been court-martialed.[*] It turned out that he didn't need to be court-martialed. He needed to have some special treatment to try to help him regain his mind. You had a terribly upset ship, and particularly in those days they didn't send much talent to the service force.

Q: I've heard that before.

Admiral Michaelis: Besides my learning what was going on, there was a lot to be done to patch the ship up and get them living as an organized group again. They had really just been through a terrible period.

Q: How long had they endured that? How long had he been sick?[†]

---

[*] The USS Tolovana (AO-64) was commissioned on 24 January 1945. She was 553 feet long, 75 feet in the beam, had a draft of 32 feet, and displaced 25,440 tons fully loaded. She had a top speed of 18 knots and a cargo capacity of more than six million gallons of fuel oil.

[†] Captain David S. Edwards, Jr., USN, commanded the Tolovana from 8 August 1958 to 11 February 1959. Lieutenant Commander Robert M. Hughson, USN, was temporary skipper from 11 February to 4 March 1959, when Michaelis took command. Captain Edwards retired 1 July 1960.

Admiral Michaelis: Well, it was a little over a year. This was the senior man in the service force. So he had a deal of--what shall I say?--a longer period before it was apparent to his superiors that his elevator didn't go to the top floor.

Q: And so it was tragic.

Admiral Michaelis: It was a very difficult period. It was a real challenge, and I must say I didn't think I would, but I enjoyed it. But, gee, I came close to clashes of all sorts. I think I would have needed another year to have sorted out and gotten a crew aboard that I would consider I could have confidence in. I knew the key people that I could count on, but there were not enough of them to take care of all the duties.

Q: Your experience so often seems to have been telescoped.

Admiral Michaelis: Well, I don't think that was just mine. That period--from after the Korean War and up to the '60s--was sort of characterized by people having short tours of duty.

Q: The Navy was sort of rudderless almost, in a sense.

Admiral Michaelis: It was a tough time for the Navy; it really was. They went through some bad ones, but I think the Navy went through a period in the '50s where they didn't know they really were not in very good shape. But they had some fine people help pull them out of it.

Q: Wasn't it discouraging also in terms of some of the men didn't see any future and wanted to get out?

Frederick H. Michaelis #3 - 83

Admiral Michaelis: Oh, yes. We had it very difficult. I remember as air group commander we had a very, very difficult time with retention. It was about as bad as any time I can think of during that period.

Q: Did you master the techniques of refueling at sea?

Admiral Michaelis: Oh, yes. I believed I could handle the thing very well, but I can recall when I was exiting the Western Pacific I went to see the Pacific Fleet Service Force Commander, who was a two-star admiral at Pearl. I went in to see him, and he asked me how I liked being an oiler skipper. I said, "Well, it's about the most humbling experience I have ever had." You know, I had always been around bigger ships and so forth. I said, "One thing I am absolutely convinced of--being the CO of any service force ship is a job; it's not a position." I'm dead certain I'm right about that.

Q: What was the tonnage of the Tolovana?

Admiral Michaelis: Loaded it was pretty close to 27,000 tons. It was practically five pounds when it was unloaded. [Laughter]

Q: You mean it bobbed around?

Admiral Michaelis: Yes. I can remember pumping it out and cleaning the tanks, and my bow was out of the water. That was the same class of tankers that was later jumboized, you know, where they took a section out of the middle of them and made them bigger. They didn't do this with the Tolovana, which was the ship I was assigned to.

So then I joined Rickover, and I just spent a year learning the ins and outs of operating nuclear power plants.

Q: This was with the idea of taking the Enterprise?

Admiral Michaelis: Yes, and I went through it right alongside the first CO; I was the alternative. Then the first exec was there. The three of us were shoulder to shoulder going through this whole course. Then I bifurcated off. When Vince de Poix went to the ship, I went to a tour of duty in strategic plans in OpNav and waited my turn, which was two and a half years.

Q: How long were you with Rickover?

Admiral Michaelis: About a year.

Q: Tell me about that. That must have been intensive.

Admiral Michaelis: Well, it was periods of high intensity punctuated with considerable boredom. The high intensity was when we would go out to the national reactor test site out at Arco, Idaho, and work in the reactor prototype. They had a Westinghouse prototype out there that was pretty close-almost identical--with the plant with one pair of reactors. They had eight reactors in Enterprise, and this was one-quarter of the plant. They operated this thing, and they improved it. They used it both for training and for engineering improvement programs.

Rickover was anxious to make sure that we were properly indoctrinated, so when we went out there, we were different than the other students, really. They took families out, and they lived in Arco or some other surrounding towns, and it was not an easy thing. They took a bus ride about 50 miles every day in to the plant and back out. We went to the plant, and we lived in a little Quonset hut and did what they call double shifting. We worked 16 hours a day, and we were off eight. We did this for a month, and then we'd go back.

Q: And join your family.

Admiral Michaelis: Go back to Washington, and we would live there. And Rickover used that period for his prospective COs to try to get them indoctrinated into his way of seeing things, as well as trained. It's not all that bad.

Q: It called for very little personal life. It was completely dedicated to the task.

Admiral Michaelis: When we got back there, there were times when he didn't expect you--we had working hours when other people had working hours. We used to hang around until 5:00 or 6:00 o'clock and sometimes when we were back there--not out at Arco--there wasn't all that much to do.

I had a couple of interesting experiences where Rickover insisted that I fly to one place or another. Getting into a small airplane with Rickover leaves a lot to be desired. He is a very impatient man, and he doesn't understand the rigidity of the instrument flight rules and so forth that you're under.

Q: Let's short-circuit them.

Admiral Michaelis: Yes. And, of course, he never asked you to fly him someplace unless he found that the airlines would take him all day to get there because of bad connections and so forth. He never flew in naval aircraft; that was a fetish of his. The first time he asked me to fly him someplace, I said, "Why don't I just call Admiral Pirie, and we'll get a flight set up."* He didn't want any part of that.

Those were long, sort of interesting little dialogues I had with the admiral. I got to know him pretty well and, like anything else, I had a great deal of respect for the kinds of things he had done. But I found him very, very difficult to be around. I don't think anybody found him comfortable to be around. I can't speak about Mrs. Rickover; she might be one

---

* Vice Admiral Robert B. Pirie, Jr., USN, served as Deputy Chief of Naval Operations (Air) from 26 May 1958 to 1 November 1962. His oral history is in the Naval Institute collection.

exception. But I don't know about that, either. But I must say I learned an awful lot from Rickover and the way he did things.

Q: And had respect for his careful approach to things.

Admiral Michaelis: I did. Rickover is a real patriot--no question about it, in my mind. One time I was complaining or telling him I disagreed with him about some generalization he had made which was pretty wild. And I said, "I'd like to go on record with you, Admiral, I don't agree with that at all." I would punctuate our conversations so many times by saying, "I don't agree with this generalization, and I just won't do it."

He said, "You don't understand the art of emphasis."

He did a magnificent thing in those days of getting those prototype reactors set up there at Arco. It was a big job to make them go, a big job to get students in and out, and a big job to get the right people for instructors. He did this in the most personalized way--worked 14-15 hours a day.

Q: That's his forte, isn't it, to be very personal?

Admiral Michaelis: Yes.

So when it was all over, I went to strategic plans.

Q: This year did contribute immensely to your knowledge.

Admiral Michaelis: Yes, yes, it did. It was really an opportunity to learn a lot about some of the history of reactors and why naval reactors took the course that they did, why pressurized water was selected for a mobile--as opposed to a stationary--reactor plant. It was interesting to watch the development of the lifetime of the cores. You know, the first core in Enterprise was about two and a half years, the second was about five years, and the next one was 13 years. That technology was something that was very, very carefully nurtured and brought along in a very safe way.

When I was in strategic plans, we had just turned the year of our Lord 1960, and the Democrats had come in with Kennedy. Man, what an experience that was. Hitch, Enthoven, and McNamara arrived with the determination that maybe there was something that should be saved in the past administrations, but it should be saved only if proven to be--I'm exaggerating, but I've never seen such people.[*]

Q: An experience without equal.

Admiral Michaelis: Yes, and there were some very good things that came in during that period, but there were a lot of horrendously . . .

Q: Who was the head of strategic plans?

Admiral Michaelis: Oley Sharp, and then Wally Wendt took his place when Sharp moved down to the Pacific.[†] It was an extremely interesting tour of duty, and I never worked harder in any job in my life, longer hours.

Q: And the thrust of strategic plans at that point was what?

Admiral Michaelis: Well, it was . . .

---

[*] Charles J. Hitch served as Assistant Secretary of Defense (Comptroller) from 1961 to 1965. Alain C. Enthoven served as Deputy Comptroller and Deputy Assistant Secretary of Defense, 1961-65, and as Assistant Secretary of Defense for Systems Analysis, 1965-69. Robert S. McNamara served as Secretary of Defense from 21 January 1961 to 29 February 1968.

[†] Vice Admiral U. S. Grant Sharp, USN, served as Deputy Chief of Naval Operations (Plans and Policy), OP-06, from 1960 to 1963. Rear Admiral Waldemar F. A. Wendt, USN, was director of the Strategic Plans Division, OP-60 from 1960 to 1965.

Q: I know in the days of Arleigh Burke and Dennison, but I don't know his.*

Admiral Michaelis: The main thrust was really devoted to the conventional war and the nuclear war, broken down between those two categories. The plans and policy end of it, which had to do with the relationships of the navies to the CinCs, and to the unified and specified commanders.† You know, the Unified Command Plan was fairly new. We used to refer to the shop I was in, which was OP-605, as the "barber shop." You know, whoever had an empty chair got the next job.

Q: You had to have gray matter, though.

Admiral Michaelis: Well, I don't know if that was a requisite or not, but we did have a very loose format in there. Oley Sharp depended on 605 to sort of take the lead in a lot of things that needed to be studied.

I can remember one of the studies that I had during that period was the multinational force. It was a time when they were trying assiduously to find some way to prevent the Europeans, our NATO allies, from proliferating their weapons. They wanted so badly to find a way without giving them the finger on the trigger. One way to do this was to train crews aboard a warship that had several nationalities involved.

Q: This was a particular baby of Claude Ricketts, was it not?‡

Admiral Michaelis: I did the first study, and Claude Rickets took up the banner.

---

* Admiral Robert E. Dennison, USN, served as Supreme Allied Commander Atlantic, Commander in Chief Atlantic, and Commander in Chief Atlantic Fleet from 1960 to 1963. His oral history is in the Naval Institute collection. Admiral Arleigh A. Burke, USN, was CNO from 1955 to 1961.
† CinCs--commanders in chief.
‡ Admiral Claude V. Ricketts, USN, served as Vice Chief of Naval Operations from 1 November 1961 until his death on 6 July 1964.

Q: Oh, really?

Admiral Michaelis: Yes, following that. And my boss at the time was Bub Ward.* He made flag in that job. His last job was down at Puerto Rico as the frontier commander. But he was a submariner, and so there were some interesting things.

I can remember a few spikes in that job, and that was one of them. I was given about six people, and I was told to turn out this study in about five and a half or six weeks. We did and used some rather tortuous words that said yes, it was feasible to do this.

Q: Were you enthusiastic about it?

Admiral Michaelis: No, no. It was terribly difficult at the time to try to come to grips with something when you knew basically it would take 15 to 20 years to develop a satisfactory multinationally manned ship. Only in wartime, when you have had exiles and so forth, and you quickly jam them aboard ships of another nation or put them in ours, does this assimilation work well, and those are people sort of without a country. Now, it was feasible, and it was proven feasible on the Ricketts, you know.†

Q: The only one we did try, wasn't it?

Admiral Michaelis: DDG something.

Q: Claude V. Ricketts.

---

* Captain Norvell G. Ward, USN. Ward, who retired as a rear admiral, discussed the multinational force concept in his own Naval Institute oral history.
† For pictorial coverage of the multinational experiment, see "The Mixed-Manning Demonstration," U.S. Naval Institute Proceedings, July 1965, pages 87-103. The issue has a painting of the USS Claude V. Ricketts on the cover.

Admiral Michaelis: They changed the name to Ricketts, but I forgot what it was before that.* But it was done successfully with a great deal of effort, and it kind of wound down in its importance. The question of proliferation began to wane and, besides, it was started out on a ship that carried no nuclear weapons. It was a test ship.

We came up at that time with an idea that--next to submarines--surface ships had the greatest survivability, because they could move. The thing to do was to build modules of Polaris missiles or even Minutemen and drop them into holds of merchant ships. Then you would do a lot of things electronically and so forth to keep yourself anonymous and not always clearly recognizable, but recognizing that you could be trailed if somebody wanted to really trail you but at great expense. You could go into waters that never really had a sanctuary--such as in the Irish Sea, where it was very, very difficult for submarines to get to--and still be in missile range of the targets. So we looked at both things: the question of what kind of ship to do this on that would be low cost and get the maximum number of missiles as an adjunct to the submarine force and at the same time man them with multinational crews. Of course, that was a stupendous thing to try to do in six weeks, to look at all the aspects of what were really two jobs.

Q: I want to know how you go about a study like that.

Admiral Michaelis: Well, we went about it vigorously; that's about the only thing that I can say. I don't know that our output was all that great, but it could be interpreted in many ways, because we used such words as "feasible." What the hell does "feasible" mean?

Q: It's a weak word.

Admiral Michaelis: It really is.

A second study that went on in that time was really sort of an anomaly. There were two naval aviators that were selected to build the case for 45 SSBNs. They were not

---

* DDG-5, commissioned originally as the USS Biddle on 5 May 1962, was renamed Claude V. Ricketts on 28 July 1964.

submariners but two naval aviators, a fellow by the name of John Miller and myself. To this day, we never knew why it was done that way.

Q: Raborn had been successful.

Admiral Michaelis: I'll tell you, it was an interesting thing when first told about this and then mentioned 45 SSBNs. We had the George Washington at that time and nothing else.[*] I can remember asking, "Well, what you really mean is what are our requirements in terms of numbers."

They said, "No, 45."

And I said, "Why 45?"

And they said, "Because that's what Arleigh Burke told Congress we needed." And our requirement came out to be 45 SSBNs. And, you know, we briefed that study all up and down. I can remember LeMay getting that briefing, and I really learned an awful lot about submarines at that time.[†] Every once in a while, I'd have to go in and close the door of the submariners and say they'd have to level with me over that BS. They had to tell me the real answers to these questions. Whether I'd use them or not, I'd have to use my judgment, but they'd have to give me the right answers and not the community answers.

Well, we got 41 SSBNs, and 90% was not bad in McNamara's day.

Q: No, indeed it wasn't.

Admiral Michaelis: For the Navy.

Q: Did you have any problem with him.?

---

[*] USS George Washington (SSBN-598), the Navy's first ballistic missile submarine, went into commission on 30 December 1959. Her first patrol began in November 1960.
[†] General Curtis E. LeMay, USAF, served as Air Force Chief of Staff from 30 June 1961 to 31 January 1965

Admiral Michaelis: We must have briefed McNamara three or four times, and he'd keep sending us back for more information. People didn't really understand. They understood the effects of nuclear weapons better than they understood how they really wanted to use them. We got ourselves locked into the business of the second strike type of thing. And that lasted for years and years and years. That was the second and that was really assailed. We did all kinds of studies and papers and so forth.

Q: It was the day of monumental studies.

Admiral Michaelis: Oh, yes, it really was. You learned how to do operations analysis, you know, and we found out how to handle McNamara at his own game. I'm sure that he wanted to proceed in an honest manner, but everybody working for him didn't necessarily have a lot of access to him and so forth.

The big mistake in those days has been repeated since. You know, systems analysis is a tool of the planner, a tool of the programmer. To ever aggregate all the analysis in one spot is bound to be an arrogation of power that's just almost impossible to handle. Many people who need that kind of analysis can't get it, because it's being controlled at one point, and that's a horrendous mistake. If I had my way, I would take all of the systems analysis that I thought we needed, and I would parcel it out. I would give this directorate some and that directorate some and use it as a tool as it was designed to be.

Q: You sound like a federalist.

Admiral Michaelis: Yes, exactly. Anyway, that was an interesting period, and we lived through it.

Q: What attempt at control did Enthoven and his people exercise in this?

Admiral Michaelis: The strongest kind. It was really a very shocking thing to find that a lot of the things that you had held dear were suddenly determined by analysis to be wrong.

And some of it was good, you know. There's nothing wrong with doing good analysis, but it's extremely important to know when you are being faced with bad analysis, because there's just as much of the latter as of the former.

Q: Or when analysis is used to substantiate a decision already made.

Admiral Michaelis: That's right. Work the problem backward, and you can do that very easily. And I guess the biggest problem for systems analysis in the Navy is that it's very difficult to handle multiple capabilities. They can do straight-line, single-mission forces, but they have a terrible time with multi-mission forces. I know you've talked to many people. It was the only thing for the first couple of years that saved the Navy. They really didn't want to take us on until they had taken on the Army and the Air Force. But they got to us.

Q: They had to get rid of Anderson first, didn't they?[*]

Q: That's another thing that went on during that period that I consider myself to be quite fortunate.

Turner Caldwell and myself, under Sharp and a couple of other people, were sort of given the job of writing the rules of engagement for the Cuban quarantine.[†] That was a straight 48-hour period, I recall, of never putting our heads down. I've a great deal of admiration for a man named Turner Caldwell. His last job in the Navy, I think, was ASW czar. I don't know if you ever talked to him.

Q: No, I never did.

---

[*] Admiral George W. Anderson, Jr., USN, served as Chief of Naval Operations from 1 August 1961 to 1 August 1963. He served only one two-year term as CNO because of differences of opinion with the civilian leadership.
[†] Captain Turner F. Caldwell, USN.

Admiral Michaelis: He's a magnificent man. If you ever have a chance to talk with Turner Caldwell, you know, he would have a lot of things that are of great value to the Navy's history.

There really wasn't much to comment on there, except that writing rules of engagement in those days was a relatively new thing, and it was terribly important, because that was the beginning of the control at the highest level.

Q: What are the parameters to the rules of engagement?

Admiral Michaelis: The rules of engagement, first of all, had to do with how you handled the quarantine, how you actually made the intercepts.

Q: This involved international law, I suppose.

Admiral Michaelis: Yes. Second, it involved the defense forces, what you would do if either strike or fighter aircraft were set up in Cuba. The words "hot pursuit" were fairly new at the time. Once you were engaged, would you continue into his airspace and under what conditions were you in quarantine? What were the things to do to the limit of applications of international law to the lower levels of warlike acts? It was extremely interesting, and there was very little background in it at the time, because that was different.

Q: The request came from the White House?

Admiral Michaelis: I don't think we had to report to the White House what we considered to be acceptable rules of engagement and still operate as military forces. They did take a while to get the rules of engagement approved, and rules of engagement have been a very strong wartime mechanism since then. The more centralized the control, the higher up you have to go to get your rules of engagement approved.

Q: How well in advance of the actual crisis did this happen?

Admiral Michaelis: Very few days.

Q: Very few days.

Admiral Michaelis: As a matter of fact, one of the things that I marveled at was the magnificent secrecy with which the quarantine was put into effect. Ships were getting under way all up and down the coast on a very measured pace and then going out and forming up their groups and working their way down south the last couple of days before the quarantine was established. It was very well done with very little fore-planning. From my point of view, it was one of the Navy's finest hours, actually, how they put themselves together and how well it was done with no leaks and so forth. Suddenly we confronted the Soviets with almost a fait accompli being in position.

The time that Kennedy went on the radio and TV, a Monday night, the quarantine was essentially in place.[*] I guess the thing that amazed me most during that period was the great fear in the White House of nuclear weapons. I tend to believe that that was a most overdone thing, overexercised fear, but you can't rule people's concern and fear.

Q: I think you can trace it right back to Hiroshima, don't you?[†]

Admiral Michaelis: Yes, oh, yes. It changed the whole course of things. The world will never be the same.

Q: How do you explain the utmost secrecy in that operation, and could that be accomplished today? Could that sort be duplicated today?

---

[*] Kennedy's nationwide address was the evening of 22 October 1962.
[†] B-29 bombers of the U.S. Army Air Forces dropped atomic bombs on Hiroshima, Japan, on 6 August 1945 and on Nagasaki, Japan, on 9 August 1945. The Japanese surrendered shortly afterward.

Admiral Michaelis: Yes, I think it could be duplicated today, but there would have to be--again, at the highest level--a determination to do this, and I don't think there's any problem with it. You're just going to have to limit your information to the people who have a need to know. And it has to be of sufficient importance, whatever the event is, to convince the players that it must be kept to the degree of secrecy necessary to make it a success. I think the degree of secrecy and the worry about whether that is possible was highlighted in that Iranian rescue effort.*

The secrecy so compartmented things. I think it had a great deal to do with the lack of success. That's my personal opinion. But, yes, I think it can be done, but there's got to be a dedication to do it, you know, and you have to have a lot of people not worry about this person or that person not knowing what's going on and just take their licks when the time comes.

Q: Corky Ward was named as commander of the Second Fleet to put this thing into operation, as I remember.† His ships were already out there, but he was not told of the operation until he rode up to the White House with Dennison.

Admiral Michaelis: Dennison was the guy that really put the operation together.

Q: Magnificent man.

---

* In an effort to rescue American hostages held in Iran, on 26 April 1980 six Air Force C-130 cargo planes and eight Navy RH-53D helicopters flew to Iran with a joint-service commando team embarked. The aircraft rendezvoused at Desert One, a site 200 miles from the Iranian capital of Teheran. Because of helicopter problems, the mission was canceled. Several servicemen were killed in the futile rescue attempt.

† Vice Admiral Alfred G. Ward, USN, commanded the Second Fleet from October 1962 to August 1963. His oral history is in the Naval Institute collection.

Admiral Michaelis: That's the only time I've been around him, when we went down to see him to plan the quarantine and the rules of engagement to go with it. So those were several highlights right there during that tour of duty. Let me move on to Enterprise.

Q: She was out there waiting for you.

Admiral Michaelis: Yes, she was waiting.

Q: Were you impatient to get to her?

Admiral Michaelis: It was terrible, particularly after two years, and I wondered if it was going to take place. It did.

Q: In July 1963.

Admiral Michaelis: My first job before I took out the Enterprise was to go out to Arco, Idaho, to study the chemistry of the reactor cores and go back and prove to Rickover that there was enough life in those chemistry cores not to bring that ship in that first year to be recored. So I saved myself a year of operation on that ship before I had to go in for the terrible job of getting it recored.

Q: Was the evidence so secure that he . . . ?

Admiral Michaelis: Well, he was being extremely conservative, you know, and he really didn't need to be. The last part of the operational life of those reactors was when we went around the world and as we came back. The control was getting a little sloppy but was perfectly safe.

Q: When you took the helm, can you contrast the operation of the Enterprise with, say, the Randolph?

Admiral Michaelis: Well, it's like night and day, from an operational point of view. The ship was terribly responsive. In a conventional ship you build up steam and you get your superheat on and so forth, and you kind of regiment it. In a nuclear reactor you had no superheat. It was all wet steam. You spin that throttle just as fast as you want to spin, and you watch the pressurizer. The responsiveness of a nuclear reactor to low-level fission in producing all this heat is very, very responsive, and there the ability to accelerate is magnificent.

The ship itself was extremely maneuverable. It had four screws, and each screw kicked a rudder. So every time a new destroyer would join up, I could put him in my wake and slow down to 13 knots, which was a critical speed. At 13 knots I would signal him to follow in my wake. I would put the rudders hard over at 13 knots and have them swing way outside. Most of the times I got a message from those guys saying, "I can't believe it. I can't believe that you really turned a carrier that tightly." And it came in handy a couple of times.

I remember that Israeli liner, the Elath, apparently had a very arrogant skipper and eventually had a collision. But in the Strait of Messina it required a little special maneuvering and so forth. But it was also a very good operating ship with lots of flexibility.

When we went around the world, we had 104 airplanes aboard. Of course, the airplanes were a bit smaller then, but we really packed them aboard. I started out and relieved in the Mediterranean and completed a cruise in the Mediterranean. Then had a stint back in the United States and went back in the Mediterranean for a full six or seven months. Then we left the Mediterranean to go around the world. So that was a rather long go.

Q: Was Rickover asking for periodic reports on the operation?

Admiral Michaelis: Oh, yes. He had a bad habit of wanting to communicate privately with the reactor officer. Almost every skipper then and later on has had to make it very clear with Rickover that he was commanding officer of the ship. We were perfectly happy to have anybody communicate, but any kinds of official reports like that would go through the commanding officer. That worked after a while, and he understood that.

Q: He should have; he had been in the Navy long enough.

Admiral Michaelis: I know, but he lived in a different world. It was a great cruise. The kinds of things we learned about going around the world, there were a few interesting things that I think have some benefit. One, we got a good taste of how to make do. One of the requirements of going around the world was that we not take on any provisions of any kind. We didn't take on any aviation fuel or any food. We could bring mail aboard. Around the world we were to maintain an average speed of 26 knots when we were at sea.

Q: There were three ships, were there not?

Admiral Michaelis: Three ships: the Bainbridge, the Long Beach, and the Enterprise.[*] But at the same time, we had a very inconsistent requirement placed on us. This was to show these ships to as many people among our friends around the world as possible. So the only way we could do this and still keep steaming was to put on what we called underway visits. Before we left the Mediterranean, we took aboard four of those carrier on-board aircraft, you know, little CODs.

We would make arrangements with the next country that we were going by to fly in and pick up 32 government politicos and military people and bring them out to the ship. We put them on a grandstand up on the 13th upper level and gave them a demonstration.

Q: Stun them.

Admiral Michaelis: I just have to tell you--that was some show we put on.

---

[*] Operation Sea Orbit, involving these three ships, began at Gibraltar on 31 July 1964 and ended at Charleston, South Carolina, on 1 October.

Q: The first one you did was Morocco, was it not?

Admiral Michaelis: The first one was Morocco, and the second was the Ivory Coast. We did 24 of those things.

Q: Except you were not permitted in South Africa.

Admiral Michaelis: No, but we exchanged honors with the South African Navy in terrible weather. I just have to take my hats off to those people. I've never seen anybody operate helicopters in that type of weather off of such small ships. They were real seamen.

We suddenly found that we were using more aviation fuel than we should.

Q: Because of these demonstrations?

Admiral Michaelis: Yes. And maybe because we had no fuelers and no other carriers around, so we always had tanker aircraft up. If we got into any kind of trouble on the deck, we could tank the airplanes and sustain them and keep them going a little longer. Then we found that we were throwing away a lot of fuel when those tankers would come back aboard and would dump a lot of excess fuel. We couldn't afford that if we could never pick up any aviation fuel around the world and still carry on the demonstrations.

So, just using this as an example, we found a way to keep the tankers hot for immediate launch and not put them airborne. We did this on what was historically the safest catapult of all, the starboard forward catapult. We kept them on the catapult hot. Once we went to this thing, of course, we saved a great deal of fuel and accounted for our fuel in a much more acceptable way--acceptable to me, anyway. It was really a technique that had never really been practiced before, and it's been practiced a lot since.

An interesting thing happened over in the Roaring Forties, when we took departure from New Zealand for the Cape, to go around South America. We were in a region where the highs and lows passed through with great frequency. Because we didn't have to fuel, we cranked our speed around to the right speed to stay in a high.

Q: Clever.

Admiral Michaelis: We rode a high for eight and a half days in an area in which the weather probably should have been miserable about two-thirds of the time. We didn't have to come off of that high, so to speak, until we got to the Cape.

Q: How did you develop this idea?

Admiral Michaelis: Well, one day when I was making the weather report to Smoke Strean, I said, "You know, I've been watching the weather maps, and I know you have. It strikes me that we were doing 24 or 25 knots, and they're moving about 28 knots. Why don't we go to 28 knots and stay comfortable, particularly for the Bainbridge, which is a much smaller ship? Let's try it."* So we cranked it up, and there was beautiful sunshine, good weather.

Q: Beating the elements.

Admiral Michaelis: Beating the elements. We had to slow down to fuel and so forth. We visited only three ports: Australia, Rio, and Pakistan.

Q: Pakistan?

Admiral Michaelis: Yes, in Karachi. But it was in the middle of a monsoon, and it was a very unsatisfactory visit. Sydney was magnificent, and so was our visit in Rio. We were at the wrong time of year, trying to get a large number of poeple in Karachi in terrible weather.

---

* Admiral Strean's recollections of the around-the-world voyage are contained in his Naval Institute oral history.

Q: One question about it. Smoke felt that the Navy high command lost interest in this around-the-world tour after the death of Claude Ricketts. He really feels that he was not supported from that time on.

Admiral Michaelis: It was a miserable setup before we left. You know, I didn't really want to get into this, but we were on-again, off-again going around the world for about 30 days and almost with that frequency. Then, of course, people were getting oochy in the crew, and the families were getting terribly upset. We finally got approval.

Now, Smoke is entirely right. I didn't know that it was the advent of the loss of Claude Ricketts.

Q: He was the main backer.

Admiral Michaelis: But I'll tell you this--the CNO, Dave McDonald, was not a backer.[*] Hell of a fine guy, but he just thought this was a PR effort and didn't think we should do it. I was anxious to be there if we were going to do it. I wasn't real sure that it was the greatest thing in the world, but I was delighted that I was around if it was going to be done. But we learned a lot.

When we came back, I remember the Secretary of the Navy and the CNO came down to meet us. But it was a duty, you know. It wasn't enthusiasm. It was the notoriety to it.

Q: I tried to get McDonald to tell me that he was not in favor of it, but he wouldn't do it.

Admiral Michaelis: Oh, he wouldn't. I can tell you that. I really heard him say it. I heard him express himself on that around-the-world cruise.

---

[*] Admiral David L. McDonald, USN, served as Chief of Naval Operations from 1 August 1963 to 1 August 1967

Well, let's see. That was the end of that, and Jimmy Holloway came aboard and relieved me.* I was selected for admiral just before I left, and I went up to an R&D job in OpNav.

Q: Did you feel that your tour on the Enterprise fulfilled all your previous expectations when you were churning for a couple of years?

Admiral Michaelis: Absolutely. That's a once-in-a-lifetime experience.

Q: That was a great command?

Admiral Michaelis: It really was. There are lots of commands and lots of excitement that goes with each of them, but there was a spirit on Enterprise that was just remarkable to me. We were a show ship, but we were great operators, and that is tough. It is really tough to keep your crew psyched up, and we won the E constantly for battle efficiency. We didn't get it the year we spent part of the time in the yard, but we did when we were out. When we did the exercises, we were at the top of the list. We kept the ship clean, and when we got orders for visitors we always got them.

Q: I suppose this helped keep the crew on their toes, did it?

Admiral Michaelis: Yes, but it gets very tiresome after a while, all these visitors aboard and ready to get under way. Jack, I remember once when we went for an operational readiness inspection out of Norfolk. We went out in a very heavy fog, and whom did we have aboard? The Secretary of the Navy, his entourage, and a gang of guests. We finally got to an open place where we could lift them off by helicopter.

I always dreaded that day when we were going to fall on our face in either one or the other--in the treatment of our guests or operationally while we were under observation.

---

* Captain James L. Holloway III, USN, commanded the USS Enterprise (CVAN-65), 1965-67.

But I don't know that it ever happened. It may have happened, but I just didn't know about it.

Q: You said earlier that the cores began to lose some energy toward the end of the around-the-world trip.

Admiral Michaelis: The cores were beginning to get what they called poisoned. That means there are formed certain chemicals in the core that make it more difficult for the reactions to take place. There's not as much fuel left, and therefore the density of the action requires more control.

You see--and you've probably talked about this with somebody--a pressurized reactor is a self-controlling type of reaction. If you set the rod at a certain place and call for changes in power, the second that you open the throttle and more steam goes out, you tend to cool the reactor. As soon as it's cool, you get more reactions, more fissions per unit of time than you did when it was hot. So it immediately throws a hell of a lot of heat into the steam generators. As soon as it's up to the place where the demand is met, why, it's hot and the numbers of reactions begin to shut down. As far as a reactor is used to power a plant that has to have another control, a pressurized water reactor is a very, very fine one. Those characteristics so desirably overcome a lot of problems in having to deal with high pressures.

Q: In a long-range sense, then, what did this around-the-world trip prove to the Navy? What positive results were achieved from it?

Admiral Michaelis: I think it indirectly demonstrated the ability to move nuclear-powered forces from one place to another at high sustained speed and have them arrive at the point of combat and ready to fight. We certainly went around the world at high speed. If it hadn't been for the morale of the crew, Rickover wanted us to go around the world and never make a stop.

Q: In other words, no port?

Admiral Michaelis: No ports, just boom around the world like he did with the submarine <u>Triton</u> in the early days, ran it around the world submerged.* I think we also developed some techniques for independent cruising, based on a carrier and operating within the confines of your own deck. It was a good operation, because we didn't have anything to fall back on. We didn't have emergency fields around there. We didn't have any other deck to land on in case something happened to the deck. I don't know that it proved that you could do this in all circumstances, but it certainly said that it was feasible to operate in the conditions where you had to with single carrier task groups. That hasn't stood up too well, I think, in later years, because there are many, many different types of aircraft that you have to put aboard ships. So your concentration on the meat-and-potato areas of strike has been diluted.†

 We learned that there was a great deal of opportunity for nuclear ships to bring weather to their advantage. I know that when Jimmy Holloway had the ship out in the Tonkin Gulf, his was the last carrier to leave when a typhoon was threatening, because normally typhoons are not in the Tonkin Gulf. Reverse that northeast flow which was so devastating with the fog, and you wanted to stay as long as you could to operate offensively in those conditions. A nuclear carrier doesn't have to fuel and doesn't have to do anything but turn around and run; she can run at high speeds and sustain it. We made a fact out of the prognostications that there were strong advantages of nuclear ships, and that was the intention, but they were never publicized. Nuclear ship drivers look at them. I don't know that we proved too much, but we thought we did at the time.

---

* In the spring of 1960, the USS <u>Triton</u> (SSN-586), commanded by Captain Edward L. Beach, USN, made the first submerged circumnavigation of the world.
† In the 1970s, when the Navy did away with dedicated antisubmarine carriers, ASW planes were put aboard the large carriers, thus diminishing the portion of their air wings used for the attack role.

Q: Then in terms of image--that has to be considered, even though Rickover didn't want to . . .

Admiral Michaelis: We really did run a lot of people through with the observation of those ships. Some of those guys in togas came aboard and watched the Sidewinder fired at a flare--you know, home right in on it and explode it.* It was a great experience. I think from that point of view, there was some U.S. image that was improved.

Q: It had to be.

Admiral Michaelis: We worked very hard while it was under way at sea.

Not much up in OpNav in R&D. There was a programming and budgeting requirements office. It was a very interesting period when I had to get into a couple of studies up there, once again in submarines. I had to do a study at one time which was to determine whether or not we should help the Netherlands in their desire to operate nuclear submarines. The Minister of Defense in the Netherlands was an ex-Navy submariner.

Q: And they wanted nuclear . . .

Admiral Michaelis: They wanted nuclear-type submarines.

Q: They wanted us to supply them?

Admiral Michaelis: Yes. They wanted us to help them like we did the Brits. So I was commissioned to see whether or not the risk to our own security and our own lead in nuclear propulsion at sea--whether it was worth it or would be jeopardized. We came out deciding that it was not the thing to do. There were many reasons why not.

---

* Sidewinder is an air-to-air missile.

Q: Security?

Admiral Michaelis: Security was the most important one. The Secretary of the Navy was then Nitze.* From time to time, the Secretary of the Navy, in the normal course of discussing capability with foreign countries, found it desirable to turn around and ask if it is reasonable to do this. So that makes it interesting.

Q: How did the Dutch react to being turned down?

Admiral Michaelis: They didn't like it, but in that same study we tried to give them some alternatives for developing. That really didn't work too well, because this was the drive of one very strong character who wanted nuclear attack submarines. He had convinced the government they needed them, and that the only place they could get them was the U.S.

Q: Were they also able to afford them?

Q: Oh, I think they could have afforded them, but it would have stripped their navy out. That's the only thing they would have had in their navy. That was another thing that was, of course, in the cost of these things--not just to acquire them but to operate them.

Q: Our point of view had to be whether they would become a component of our national defense.

Admiral Michaelis: Indeed, and that, of course, entered into it. Their nuclear submarine assignments were very limited, you know. Their chunk of water and their littorals and so forth, the North Sea . . .

Q: Not very much, no.

---

* Paul H. Nitze served as Secretary of the Navy from 29 November 1963 to 30 June 1967.

Admiral Michaelis: No.

Q: We wouldn't want them going into the Baltic, I would think.

Admiral Michaelis: Perhaps you wouldn't.

Q: Did you get as far as finding out whether they'd be willing to conform to all our standards?

Admiral Michaelis: Well, they averred they would, of course. They would pony up to whatever U.S. operating standards were. The Brits did the same thing. I don't think there was much problem there as there was just being the wrong thing to do from the viewpoint of the United States on its own lead in nuclear submarines and the inappropriateness of the Netherlands, based on their role in naval warfare. It was inappropriate. They would have been much better with some little 15,000-ton ships that carried six ASW helicopters.

Q: Yes, it was reaching a little high, wasn't it?

Admiral Michaelis: Yes, and working in the North Sea, which was very shallow and where they need certain specialized kinds of ASW equipment, really becoming king of the mountain.

Q: How would it have tied in with the unionized navy too?

Admiral Michaelis: Oh, that came later, and that would have been terrible.

Q: That was not in existence then?

Admiral Michaelis: No, no, and nor was there really a hint of it. I was very taken with the Netherlands Navy--top-notch, hard-nosed officers and the leadership. I used to sit in on a couple of NATO committees during that period, and lots of people who were the best informed and did their homework best were the Dutchmen. They're awfully hard to close a deal with too--hard traders. Not much in that tour. It was an interesting period.

Interview Number 4 with Admiral Frederick H. Michaelis, U.S. Navy (Retired)

Place: The Cosmos Club, Washington, D.C.

Date: Monday, 8 March 1982

Interviewer: John T. Mason, Jr.

Q: Well, sir, it's great to see you. Let me thank you officially for the luncheon today. It was delicious.

Admiral Michaelis: I'm delighted we could finally get together. I haven't been very helpful to your schedule the last couple of efforts.

Q: Last time you talked about the around-the-world tour when you were skipper of the USS Enterprise. Then you came back in August of 1965 to Washington and became director of the development program.

Admiral Michaelis: I was in the office of the Deputy CNO for Research and Development. My job there was to cover the air programs, surface programs, electronic warfare, and a lot of hang-around cats and dogs.

Q: Was this long-range planning?

Admiral Michaelis: No, this was not. This was R&D. We had all of the R&D programming and budgeting structure there, with the exception of what they called basic research. That belonged to the Office of Naval Research. The Chief of Naval Material had what we called 6.2, which was really the basic lead-in to advanced development.

I think probably the only thing that was of special interest in this job was that at the time when I had it, we were just beginning to get deeply involved in the conflict in Vietnam.

We entered into a period of sensor development with the idea that with a limited number of people in country--of course, not wishing to exchange bodies with the Vietnamese--the U.S. had elected to try the sensor route of all sorts: seismic sensors, EW, ground, airborne, land mines, and shallow-water mines.* These were the kinds of things that would have a rapid payoff if they would be developed in that way. So it was a very busy time.

Q: Were those requests coming from the field?

Admiral Michaelis: A great many of them. We were very busy getting scientific and research and development advisers to the Pacific Fleet and out in country.†

Q: And then they reported back to you?

Admiral Michaelis: Yes. It was really the beginning of the prominence of ARPA, the Advanced Research and Development Agency organization under the Department of Defense. In fact, I think that's where it was born. It's now DARPA, Defense Advanced Research and Development Agency.

There was an expression that was very common in those days called "less than radar significant." In other words, these were the sensors that would tell you about movements. They distinguished between people and their surroundings and so forth in ways that gave you more discrimination than radar. These were things such as infrared and acoustics and so forth.

Q: How did this tie in with the Army effort?

Admiral Michaelis: They were pretty well tied together. In fact, a bit of the Army development work was done by the Navy, because what they did was adapt some Navy fuzes to various pieces of equipment. One of the things that we badly needed in those days

---

* EW--electronic warfare.
† "In country" meant ashore in South Vietnam.

and never did quite finish before the war was over was a penetration weapon which could get into the karst caves and so forth up in there, the karst formations in North Vietnam.[*]

A second thing that I recall as at least having an influence on my later years was we had just really begun to get into the computer world in the tactical arena in 1966-67.

Q: A relatively short time, isn't it?

Admiral Michaelis: Yes, it is. These computers were becoming what they called "embedded computers." In other words, they were a part of the systems but not the whole systems. Secondly, we were just beginning to introduce computers as aids to tactical commands. I remember very clearly that I learned fairly rapidly the limitations in the use of computers, because I found some of my people trying to peddle computers to such things as carrier divisions. But they really didn't have much use for them. I became very incensed at some of the efforts to try to inject computers in places where they really didn't have much use.

Q: In enthusiasm sometimes we forget they require a human mind somewhere along the line, too, don't they?

Admiral Michaelis: Absolutely.

I had an opportunity during my next tour to work with part of those things that were developed during that period or closed out of development during that period and sort of expedited into production.

Q: Let me ask how closely did you work with an outfit like NOL?[†]

Admiral Michaelis: Well, we worked very closely with NOL. We worked very closely with China Lake, which was the ordnance development and testing field activity. I did not have

---

[*] Karst is an irregular limestone region with sinks, underground streams, and caverns.
[†] NOL--Naval Ordnance Laboratory, White Oak, Maryland.

any responsibilities at that time for R&D centers or labs. That was all under NavMat, with the exception of the Naval Research Lab, which was under the Secretary.* The Navy's got a very different setup for their R&D. It's rather anachronistic. Things have been carried over from the days when it was necessary to closely safeguard some of the laboratory base in the Navy. In the early days, there was a tendency to wipe such things out that were in the active services. In the early days, the Navy's research labs were put directly under the Secretary of the Navy, and they have been carried there ever since.

Q: For protective purposes?

Admiral Michaelis: No, just because institutionalization is very resistant to change. It's always been a nice prestige item for the Secretary to have, particularly now that we have an assistant secretary for R&D. Now we call it RES--research engineering and systems. I didn't consider that we accomplished too much in that office during that period. We did a lot of juggling of budgets and so forth, trying to get a prioritization for things that we were using up. Southeast Asia . . .

Q: Did you go out to Southeast Asia yourself to facilitate things?

Admiral Michaelis: No, I never made the trip out there. I kept getting mixed up at that time with the Secretary of the Navy. For example, he interested himself at one particular point with the question of whether the Dutch should be given some aid in developing nuclear submarines. I was pulled out of my job for a month to do a study to try to determine whether or not this would have a deleterious effect from a security or other point of view--the Navy's own nuclear submarine problem.

Q: Was it related to the fact that British had made an arrangement?

---

*NavMat--Naval Material Command.

Admiral Michaelis: Yes. Of course, we shared programs with the British. In fact, we worked very closely in making it possible for them to have the capability.

It just happened that in that particular juncture in time, the Dutch Minister of Defense was an ex-submariner. He was a very persuasive gentleman, and he persuaded the Parliament over there that the most important thing the Dutch Navy could do was develop a nuclear capability. It was a very difficult thing to turn them down. So they produced a study which I did in very short order. It put the thing from two points of view. One, would it be the right thing to give them this technology from the viewpoint of the hot competition that was going on between the Soviet Union and the U.S. Navy? Two, whether it was even the right thing for them to develop in a community of nations over there. Was it the right kind of weapon for them to develop? The answer was "no" on both of them.

Q: So the study was the turndown?

Admiral Michaelis: The study was the turndown. Paul Nitze was the Secretary, and we got some chestnuts in the fire a little later in trying to soothe the Dutch. We suggested that they pursue a propulsion system called "fuel cells." It was just like the ones that they later used in space, except they were gargantuan and power producers in large quantity. The only people that were doing that were working with the Swedes. So I spent some time in Sweden. Then I had to write a report to the Secretary on whether or not it had a future that didn't involve expending so much funds that it really couldn't be amortized over the benefits of the program. The answer that I came back with was that it was a very dangerous thing to put into submarines. A little later on, the big fuel cell blew up in Sweden.

In thinking about the time I spent in Sweden, one of the other things comes to mind. The Swedish were building a fighter attack plane that was called the Beacon 37. It was one of the first airplanes that had a canard surface up forward. The reason that the U.S. Navy was consulting with the Swedes over the Beacon 37 was that it was being designed to land on roads and other temporary type of strips. These led back into their mountain recesses and so forth where they stored quite a bit of their system there. I guess it's fairly common knowledge that they have done a lot with their mountains up there, a few things of defense. Maybe it isn't; I don't know.

They wanted to land at slow speed. Of course, the Navy has been landing high-performance aircraft at low speed on carriers for a long time, so they asked us for some help. I had the opportunity to go to a Saab factory there where they were making this. That was interesting, if not necessarily productive.

Q: Did they adapt to any of our ideas?

Admiral Michaelis: Oh, yes. They were well down the road. That forward canard is a very fine way to get additional lift in the positive sense. They applied it very well, I think. The Beacon was a successful bird. It was probably a little too expensive to command a market, but, nevertheless, it's always been considered a fine airplane by people who know airplanes. So that was more under the heading of enjoyment and fun than anything else.

Q: You might make the general statement as to the enrichment of our efforts in various directions as they come from foreign countries like Sweden and U.K.

Admiral Michaelis: At that time I worked on a NATO committee which was called the naval armaments committee. It was a tremendously interesting experience. All the NATO members met twice a year.

Q: Was this under the aegis of the military committee?

Admiral Michaelis: Yes, that's right, the military committee. It was the road to a lot of exchange programs. It didn't amount to very much in the way of showing programs, but during that period we were looking very hard to set up a showcase program, a joint effort between the United States and the NATO countries. I did get the NATO Sea Sparrow program going at that time with, I have to say, a great deal of effort.* It's been a very successful program and, in fact, one that's been sort of a standout in the years past. Norway was in it, the Netherlands, Italy. This was an adaptation of the U.S. Sea Sparrow to a NATO environment.

Q: What were some of the handicaps you dealt with?

Admiral Michaelis: The biggest handicap at that time was that the difference between the technical and manufacturing base of the European countries and the United States was so broad that it was difficult to get a reasonable cost program unless it was all done by the United States. That's a terrible setback when you're trying your best to do joint work. So the reason we settled on the Sea Sparrow as a surface-to-air missile adapted from an air-to-air missile was that it had already enjoyed some success in the United States. But there were certain adaptations to Dutch ships and to Norwegian ships that had to be done. So they were relatively simple things being done overseas in contribution to this weapon. They were low cost; they were things that could be done. But I enjoyed attaching the NATO name to it.

Q: Yes.

Admiral Michaelis: That's what I was looking for.

Q: The subject of standardization, I suppose, was very large.

Admiral Michaelis: Yes. In fact, it was right along in that period that, where it made more sense, the term "interoperability" came along as an alternative to standardization.

---

* Sea Sparrow is a surface-to-air missile.

So those were some of the highlights. It was a very busy two years. I was constantly jumping from one thing to another. It was a terrible period from the viewpoint of the F-111 in those days. I was the witness in Congress for the F-111.

Q: Oh, were you really?

Admiral Michaelis: I really knew nothing about it, because the program was totally run by the Secretary.

Q: Tom Connolly could brief you, couldn't he?*

Admiral Michaelis: Later on. I was in the early days of the F-111, when we were trying to get together on a joint program.† It was very painful. In fact, I can remember I had just been selected for admiral, but I wasn't wearing the cap and stripes. One of the gentlemen I was witnessing, who I guess was in the Appropriations Committee, looked over the edge of his desk and said, "Mike, would you just like to have me hold this testimony up until you're sure you're putting on your stripes?"

Q: He knew. Tell me more about that in your participation. That, of course, is historic.

Admiral Michaelis: My participation was very, very minimal. I simply carried the Navy form. Nitze was the Navy's member of the joint team under Brown and headed up by McNamara. I just have to say in the greatest candor that it was a very, very closed system.

Q: All like minds, weren't they?

---

* Vice Admiral Thomas F. Connolly, USN, served as Deputy Chief of Naval Operations (Air) from 1 November 1966 to 31 August 1971. Admiral Connolly's oral history is in the Naval Institute collection.
† The F-111--originally designated TFX--was a controversial fighter plane that Secretary of Defense Robert McNamara tried to develop in the 1960s for use by both the Air Force and the Navy.

Admiral Michaelis: Yes.

Q: And how could you accommodate yourself to that closed system?

Admiral Michaelis: Well, it was obvious in the testimony that I gave that it was strictly ho-hum. If you really wanted to get the answer on these things, you had to go to the Secretary and get it. They used to ask me some very interesting questions, and then they got over doing that. They just didn't do it after a while. They said we had to go through this thing and pursue this in another manner.

Q: I take it the attitude of the congressional committees was not very enthusiastic?

Admiral Michaelis: No, it wasn't. Then, of course, when Tom Connolly came along a couple of years after that, he broke the code. He just got in a place where he couldn't go on, because pretty soon we were going to have to put those airplanes aboard a carrier, and then the whole world was going to know it was just not a suitable carrier airplane.

Q: His testimony constituted the denouement, didn't it.

Admiral Michaelis: Yes, it did.
    Well, shortly after that, I went to Vietnam as commander of Carrier Division Nine.

Q: Yes, this was in December of 1967. Was this something you had been angling for?

Admiral Michaelis: Well, of course, I was angling for it. I was terribly anxious to get out there.

Q: For a carrier division?

Admiral Michaelis: Yes. Gee, we worked every weekend, and on a Saturday afternoon I got a call from Mickey Weisner, who said, "Would you like a cardiv?"[*]

I said, "Is the Pope a Catholic?" or something like that.

He said, "How about a week from Tuesday?" I'm not exaggerating. That's what he said. So I closed up my affairs in a week, and I did get an extra week when I drove my family to the West Coast. I was in Vietnam within a month of the time when I was first informed and had relieved.

Q: Whom did you relieve out there?

Admiral Michaelis: I relieved Admiral Walt Curtis.[†] He went to the Pacific Fleet staff at that point.

Of course, during this period in the last part of 1967 and the early part of '68 . . .

Q: Coming up to the Tet offensive?

Admiral Michaelis: Yes. We were at that point of the war where we were working over only designated targets. The rest of the time we were trying to cut out the routes farther to the south. It was a very, very frustrating period. I will say that I worked very hard from the time I left there to try to get more Walleyes in theater. Walleye was the TV bomb that was a glide job. The shallow-water mine was new. That was just a 500-pound bomb with a special anti-disturbance type of fuze on it.

The North Vietnamese became very sharp bridge builders. We found that we could knock down a bridge, and overnight they would build it up--rickety as it might be--to get parts, bicycles, and so forth across. Then by dawn's early light they'd fold it back so that it

---

[*] Rear Admiral Maurice F. Weisner, USN, Assistant Chief of Naval Personnel for Personnel Control.
[†] Rear Admiral Walter L. Curtis, Jr., USN.

still appeared to be a destroyed bridge. So we developed a technique there that we called "strike mine." We were, of course, husbanding our Walleyes, because we encountered them with twos, fours, and sixes. They were coming just in the early stages of pilot production. We would launch a strike group of one airplane with Walleye on it and the rest of them with mines. We could knock a bridge out and then immediately mine it. It was fairly effective for at least several days for holding a route without bridges on it.

Q: Did these operations have to be on orders from Washington too?

Admiral Michaelis: No, not these. These were the route control--the ones with the major targets that we struck, targets in the vicinity of Haiphong--the power plants--and in the vicinity of Hanoi. Everything was complicated, of course, by foreign ships and particularly the Chinese being in Haiphong Harbor. The inability to take out all of the supplies that were stacked up around the harbor, because it was obvious how they were handling their areas of sanctuary from our bombing. It was very frustrating.

Then, when you combine that with the problems of the northeast monsoons, when they'd set in in the wintertime. You'd have a very, very low strata for days and weeks on end. It was, as I say, a very frustrating time.

Q: Did you have your flagship in the Tonkin Gulf?

Admiral Michaelis: Yes, in the Tonkin Gulf. The USS Oriskany, for the most part, was my flagship. Then later it was the USS Hancock. CarDiv 9 was in the smaller carriers, which had an absolutely wonderful Avis approach to things.* They were never to be outdone by the big carriers. They would launch faster, recover faster, and carry as big a load. When we'd go to Yokosuka or someplace, they'd advertise that fact.

Q: Did you encourage that spirit?

---

* The motto of the number-two rental car company, Avis, was "We try harder."

Admiral Michaelis: Of course.

Q: What about the Yankee Station task group that you also had under your control?

Admiral Michaelis: Yankee Station, of course, was a mythical area out in the water north of a certain latitude in the Tonkin Gulf. The carrier division commanders were assigned as Yankee team commander in rotation, so to speak. If you had two of them out there, you were Yankee team commander half the time. If there were three out there, a third of the time. It really was a pretty good way of doing things. During the time you were Yankee team commander, you were in charge of the air defense of the gulf. You were in charge of sequencing and the timing of the strikes, the sizes of the strikes. You were on the receiving end of all the authorities that were passed in the gulf to do certain things.

Q: How were the communications with Washington in terms of instructions?

Admiral Michaelis: The communications themselves were necessarily good.

Q: They didn't break down?

Admiral Michaelis: What was communicated was not very good. Well, there were breakdowns. There were breakdowns in some very fortuitous times, as a matter of fact. [Laughter]

Q: Talk about your pilots and safeguarding them from capture and that sort of thing.

Admiral Michaelis: I guess the greatest unsung heroes of that particular conflict were the helicopter pilots that seemed to go almost anyplace and pick up--if they were able to operate soon enough. Their biggest problem was that they were slow. They were not in the proximity of the strike group, so there was a hysteresis in getting them in there, making the decision that if the pilot was down in an area, knowing where he was and so forth, to be able to profitably send in a helicopter to get him. The beepers worked very well. The instructions to the pilots were good. Considering the kind of equipment they had to deal with, I think they did a very good job of pulling pilots out.

We had always designated, of course, what we called safe areas or the rescue area. So if there was anything you could do to maneuver yourself to the area or steer your kite to that area, you would do so. There was an area always that was proposed because it had the highest probability of lowest concentration of either military or inhabitants.

Q: You did have difficulty in an adequate supply of helicopters, though, didn't you?

Admiral Michaelis: Well, the Navy didn't have much trouble. The Army did; they lost a lot of helicopters.

Q: I mean in getting helicopters for your use. I was told that certainly in the delta area, they just cried for helicopters and the Navy couldn't get them.*

Admiral Michaelis: Yes. The Navy had a couple of helicopter squadrons ashore that were called HAL squadrons--helo attack light. They were lightweight attack helicopters. They didn't have trouble keeping those people supplied. They were supporting the riverine warfare in the delta. They lost a lot of them. They were pretty elite helicopter organizations. They were the ones that everybody wanted to get into. They were the helicopter pilots that came out of the war with a lot of decorations.

I later on had an aide who was a HAL pilot and had a whole chest full of medals that other helicopter pilots didn't have. The helicopter organizations that I saw, of course, were simply the logistic and ASW.

Q: You were telling me about where they came from--the Army originally.

---

* This is a reference to the Mekong River delta in South Vietnam.

Admiral Michaelis: Bell had developed this helicopter for the Army, and it was a gunship.* The Navy got as many as they could, and they outfitted these support squadrons. They were supporting the Swift river boats and the riverine forces of the delta. They did a lot of night work; they did a lot of stealth work and so forth. I really don't know too much about shortages, but I'm sure there were some, because everybody was trying to get their hands on gunships.

Q: How did your command, the carriers, tie in with the riverine warfare people?

Admiral Michaelis: None.

Q: None whatsoever? You had nothing to do with the Swift boats either?

Admiral Michaelis: No. That was way down at the south. It was sort of the protection of using the river systems of the south to supply the Viet Cong. We didn't have anything to do with it. We were operating entirely to the north, along with the Air Force.

Q: Did you have any concern for the possibility of enemy submarines in the area?

Admiral Michaelis: No, we didn't, although we constantly kept the area sanitized. The Tonkin Gulf is relatively shallow, at least from the viewpoint of the depth that submarine operators like to operate submarines. I'm judging from our own; I'm assuming there's some replication of the desires of submarines of other nations not to involve themselves in shallow water. Now, on the other hand, I'm sure there was a lot of recon done with very slow-moving battery-type submarines that would lie in one spot for a long time.†

---

* The Army version was the AH-1G HueyCobra; the utility version used by the Navy and Marine Corps was the UH-1 Iroquois.
† Recon--reconnaissance.

Q: Their identity would be Russian?

Admiral Michaelis: Could be Russian, could be Chinese, mostly Russian. And, of course, we kept track of it pretty well in the approaches to the gulf. There were always Russian submarines operating in the approaches.

Q: And trawlers too?

Admiral Michaelis: Oh, yes, a lot of trawlers in the gulf.

Q: I mean Russian trawlers.

Admiral Michaelis: Yes.

Q: Spy trawlers.

Admiral Michaelis: Electronic vacuum cleaners.

Q: Ever present.

Admiral Michaelis: We had a very short tour of duty in OP-05. I carried Tom Connolly's sword; I was OP-05B.

Q: Elaborate on what that was, the sword.

Admiral Michaelis: I was his deputy, and I acted for him when he was gone, which was a good part of the time. I had oversight duties in general of the air warfare world, and I had some specific duties which he handed off to me. I became very familiar with the air reserve at that time. I found it to be fascinating.

Q: That was building, was it?

Admiral Michaelis: That was building, and what I took on as my job was to try to improve the responsiveness of the air reserve. In simple terms, should they be called on, we didn't want to spend many months getting them ready. They could go in a very short allocated period of time and be carrier-qualified and ready to go.

Q: Their state of readiness was in the reserve.

Admiral Michaelis: Yes, they were reserve squadrons. The first thing we had to do was get their equipment more operational than it had been in the past.

Q: You mean comparable to what they must use on active duty?

Admiral Michaelis: Yes, and the ability to use the weapon systems.

Q: It's a major operation.

Admiral Michaelis: It's one thing just to fly the airplane and expect to go into another airplane as a reserve when you go into combat. It's quite another if you take your own equipment to combat. So those were busy times. I got to know the reserves. I got a good understanding of how the reserve thinks.

Q: Approximately how many reserves did you have in the air reserves?

Admiral Michaelis: We had somewhere pretty close to 20,000.

Q: Scattered all over the country?

Admiral Michaelis: Yes. They concentrated for their weekend drills at several reserve air stations and reserve units that were on reserve fields from other services. The air reserve or the Air National Guard, as well as Naval Reserve people. There was a lot of consolidation going on at that point, closing down the fields that were common to highly dense urbanized areas and consolidating at one or the other fields of the particular service for conservation purposes.

Q: This entailed a lot of expense, did it not? Were the funds forthcoming readily?

Admiral Michaelis: No, actually it was to save the dollars that all of this was being done.

Q: I mean the equipment.

Admiral Michaelis: It was coming easier than it had in the past. There was some question about whether we'd have to use it or not, so there was equipment becoming available at the lower end of the spectrum. The A-4s were coming into the reserves as A-7s came into the fleet, and we managed to get the first squadrons of F-4s in there. They were flying only F-8s at the time. So, generally speaking, this was sort of an upgrading. I don't know why I'm dwelling on that, because it was a very, very small part of what I had to do.

Q: But an interesting one, however. What about the morale?[*]

---

[*] Interview 4 ended at this point because of background noise and confusion in the Cosmos Club. The discussion of Admiral Michaelis's duty in OP-05 continues in interview 5.

Interview Number 5 with Admiral Frederick H. Michaelis, U.S. Navy (Retired)

Place: Naval Historical Center, Washington, D.C.

Date: Wednesday, 21 April 1982

Interviewer: John T. Mason, Jr.

Q: Take up the cudgels, Admiral. At this point you came back from Vietnam, and in August of 1968 you were given an assignment in OP-05B. As you say, you were the sword carrier for Tom Connolly.

Admiral Michaelis: There really was not anything very auspicious about that one year I spent there. I learned a lot about the naval air reserves.

Q: Well, that's something worthwhile.

Admiral Michaelis: Tom Connolly walked in one day, threw a bunch of papers on my desk, and said, "I give up. From here on out, you're going to have the naval air reserve responsibility in this office." I found it to be very challenging, and I also found out that the naval air reserve was an extremely important element of our total defense fabric--at least the Navy's defense fabric. Given the right equipment, they were magnificent performers, and they very seldom got the right equipment.

I think the direction has gone since that time of making what we call "one Navy." The one-Navy concept is extremely important, and I'm not sure that the reserves all understand that approach. It's very difficult for them to understand it and to be practitioners of the reserve arts. Of course, there are an awful lot of little cells of interest and so forth that make it difficult to put things together. But if one is willing to work with the reserves and understand their limitations and exploit what they have in the way of potential, they can be a very, very important part. I'm not speaking across the board on reserves, because my only experience is with the air reserves.

Q: They're not laggards, by any means.

Admiral Michaelis: No, and they're a great source of war-fighting capability when you need them. They would be an extremely important part, if that one bugaboo of not being able to call them up without a national emergency could be overcome. If there was some kind of a ready force in the reserves in which the employers understood that for any given year something like one-fourth of the reserve was on a ready status, which meant that you didn't have a national callup. Employers would have to accept for that coming year that they would be called up during the year for an emergency in which they became part of the deterrent system and not just the war-fighting system. They could be very, very important to this country. Some day I think we're going to have to come to something like that.

Q: How would you go about that? It's a matter of education, isn't it?

Admiral Michaelis: Yes, it's a matter of education. It's a matter of being needed. It's a matter of recognizing that, given the right equipment, the cost of maintaining air reserves is about 30% or 40% of what it costs to keep a regular Navy squadron. If a certain portion of those were callable without a national emergency, it would be a grand signal to send to somebody that you're calling up the ready reserve and putting them in position. And that term "ready reserve" would have a special connotation that says maybe it's 25% or 30% of the total reserve. In maybe two months you will put them right back again. It would be a very simple system of doing this. The Israelis don't do badly at this at all. As things get more and more expensive, the United States may have to do the same kind of thing. I think the ready air reserve is one in which you'd get a lot of benefit out of it.

Q: Doesn't this involve up-to-date equipment for their training?

Admiral Michaelis: Of course it does.

Q: You can't have obsolete planes.

Admiral Michaelis: That's right. And that's something that I'm delighted to see. Now that we have a reserve as the Secretary of the Navy, he is making a real try for modern equipment.[*] In fact, he's made the statement amongst the reserves that within three years there will be a reserve F-18 squadron. I hope he's right.

Q: He's a pretty determined young man.[†]

Admiral Michaelis: That he is, I know. Anyway, that's one of the things I got a little insight into.

Q: Wouldn't this call for some legislation in order to put this in effect?

Admiral Michaelis: Oh, absolutely.

Q: Then perhaps you have to work on Congress.

Admiral Michaelis: You do. First of all, the Navy's got to want to do this badly enough. I'm looking for all kinds of things in terms of MSC forces, as well as reserve forces where you have some contingency money available to put that into a deterrent.[‡] Make them part of the deterrent system, not just the war-fighting system. War-fighting systems are best when they're both. The only way to be a credible deterrent is to be a credible war-fighter, but you have to have some freedom to use your war-fighting forces to make them credible deterrents. We don't use the reserves that way. We should have some portion of the

---

[*] John F. Lehman, Jr., served as Secretary of the Navy from 1981 to 1987.
[†] Lehman, who was born 14 September 1942, was 38 years old when he took office on 5 February 1981.
[‡] MSC--Military Sealift Command.

reserves that we can use without a national emergency. Just like we should start loading ships without a national emergency, even if we have to unload them and it costs us a few hundred thousand dollars to do that. It's one of the greatest forms of deterrence that I know of.

Q: But aren't we moving in that direction with this mobile force?

Admiral Michaelis: We are, simply because our long fascination with NATO now has been forced into another part of the world. So you have to do something special like this in order to be timely. With sea forces, since you don't preposition tons and tons of equipment, with no place to preposition it except at sea, then you must eventually find some way to move rapidly at sea. The only way you do that is to get started faster than you would otherwise. The only way you do that is to get away from the elements that make up the total delay package. The one that's the most significant in that is the political, and something has to be done about this if you're going to make it successful.

Q: You have the element of the convenience of the families of these men when they are called out.

Admiral Michaelis: Tough.

Q: The disruption which we witnessed in the Berlin Crisis.[*]

Admiral Michaelis: Yes, but you see, we never positioned ourselves. Out of a four-year period for a man in the reserves, he should set out two six-month periods or one one-year period in which he can expect to be called up without a national emergency. His employer knew that, his family knew it. Nine times out of ten he's not going to get called up, but he

---

[*] In July 1961 President John F. Kennedy announced a "call to arms" that involved, among other things a callup of 250,000 reservists for a one-year term of service and the reactivation of a number of reserve fleet ships.

has an obligation. No crying, scream, wailing, and so forth. You just go. You'll find a lot of support among the reserves for this sort of thing.

Q: I would not be surprised.

Admiral Michaelis: You won't find it total, of course. And you'll find less support among the industry of the United States to stomach something like this. But you have to start planning around it. The people that they're going to call up to bring into their work force, because it's a time of national crisis, have got to be different people. These people for this one-year period are going to be called up because they, for sure, are going to be the first ones. They're going to have an element of dollars added, both in terms of pay and training for that year. It's going to be more than their reserve confreres who are not in that status. That is the way I look at it. Now, let's see, what else did I do?

Q: That was a valuable lesson to learn while you were spending time in OP-05.

Admiral Michaelis: I think that there's a lot of potential we're not tapping. This just happens to be one of my very conservative feelings about what goes on these days. I have the feeling that we've had so many people tell us that we should not be dedicated, in my view, that it's almost a sense of relief when the country has a little change of heart like it's had in the last couple of years. It's almost a sense of relief to a great many people. That's philosophy.

Q: Then they'd better pull up their breeches and support it.

Admiral Michaelis: I agree. And I think we're going to see a little bit more of this. It's going to take us so long to get over where we are now--the idea of getting it over in the course of one administration is just not going to do it. We have a long way to go, and I hope to God we stay firm in the directions we're taking.

Let's see. The other things that happened in 05 while I was there--we did a great deal of expediting, trying to get things on a butter-and-bullets basis in this country, trying to get things out to Southeast Asia that we needed. There were all kinds of compromises made, of course, during that period of 1968-69, around in that area where we have been suffering for 15 years since then. Compromises were made in tools of war in order to get munitions of war in hand to expend at a very high rate. So we spent a great deal of our time doing that, not particularly fruitful at times.

Q: Were you concerned about the waste that is concurrent with that?

Admiral Michaelis: Well, the kind of war we were fighting invited waste. It was a go-nowhere war, and you can't fight a war day after day on a go-nowhere basis and not have almost everything wasted, in my opinion.

The time came to leave, and I went out to the JSTPS.

Q: That was an interesting assignment, one that many men have said they'd just as soon skip, however.

Admiral Michaelis: It was interesting. Well, it's an element that's necessary to make credible your national nuclear deterrent. If you had, as we did at one time, a great many weapons coming in from various sources and you didn't have some kind of a plan to integrate them all, not only would you be very foolish not to have an integrated plan, but you would encourage the enemy to recognize that you had no plans, that you had no direction of where you were going and so forth. The problem with all of this is that you have to, because nobody has any experience in nuclear weapons--nobody. We have no experience in the use of nuclear weapons, and that's very good. But it does make the planning difficult. Everything comes to a statistical probability.

Q: And even a bit of surmise, I suppose.

Admiral Michaelis: Any world that's based totally on statistical probability has got some flaws in it. But I will say this--I spent two years out there trying to find a better way to do the SIOP, and I never found it.* I think some people before me have tried to do the same thing and probably some after me. But, you know, as fighting people, it's very difficult to play with these statistical figures that you're using. You almost play like they're real life. You use them as though they were real life and use them for the justification of weapons and the kinds of weapons you use. You use them for justification of distribution of weapons, the balance between the legs of the triad and so forth.

Q: I guess when you live with it from day to day, you have to.

Admiral Michaelis: Yes, it's like anything else, like building the bridge over the River Kwai.† I don't want to say that you get brainwashed with this thing, but you are very careful to stand back and look at it hard from time to time. That's the danger of anything--if it's a massive system in which you have rather elegant plans, you hope you'll never have to use them, hope against hope, for more reasons than one.

Q: And if you do have to use them, you hope you won't be surprised by the fact that they don't work.

Admiral Michaelis: That's right. I think that sometimes the SIOP is advertised as a very, very rigid plan. It has its flexibilities, and I would say that there's a lot of people working hard to give the country and the national command authority as much leeway as they can in how they would use their weapons. I think they do a pretty damn good job. I'll say this

---

* SIOP--Single Integrated Operational Plan.
† The building of a Japanese railroad in Burma and Siam in World War II was the subject of a 1957 movie titled The Bridge on the River Kwai.

straight--in those days; it's probably not the case now--I had thought that the locale for the JSTPS should have been someplace other than in the same underground with SAC.*

Q: You mean it's too much Air Force?

Admiral Michaelis: Well, it was very difficult. You see, a tremendous portion of the staff was double-hatted for economy purposes. I think that in many cases it was the right thing to do, but it tended to be very slow to recognize the proper employment and capabilities of forces other than Air Force forces. It took place, it happened, it's in good shape, I think, now.

Q: I was about to ask how large a naval contingent did you have out there when you were there?

Admiral Michaelis: I don't know. The Air Force had by far the biggest, and then there was the Navy/Marines and then the Army. Those are sort of the relative sizings. I can't tell you the numbers. I would guess maybe, including the representatives of the CinCs, that we had out there maybe 35 or 40 naval officers. Probably also the same amount of Army, a double handful of Marines, and all the rest of them were Air Force. I learned a lot about strategic things and how people operate in the strategic world. We had an opportunity to see the inside of the CinC's organizations which we wouldn't have otherwise.

Q: And, incidentally, what do the reps contribute to the wisdom there in the outfit?

---

* The Joint Strategic Target Planning Staff and the Strategic Air Command were located at Offutt Air Force Base near Omaha, Nebraska.

Admiral Michaelis: I think the reps system in JSTPS is probably pretty good. With the exception of some ultra-inner sanctum things, they have a constant and thorough look at the SIOP, and they have an opportunity to make both inputs and withdrawals, so to speak--withdrawals being information of SIOP that they send back to their boss, saying they like this or don't like it type of thing. I think the rep system worked pretty well out there. The rep system in any place works well, depending on two things: the kind of people you send out there and what you expect of them.

Q: People, always people.

Admiral Michaelis: Always people. I guess my next job was the best job I had in all my career.

Q: Before you go to the next job, tell me about how you settled into the Nebraska life.

Admiral Michaelis: Nifty.

Q: You liked that?

Admiral Michaelis: Loved it.

Q: Because you're Middle West.

Admiral Michaelis: I am, and I had forgotten how great they are. I really had. I had been away from the Middle West so long that I had forgotten how pleasant it is to be amongst those in the Middle West, in my view.

Q: Lacking the pressure of the East to a certain extent.

Admiral Michaelis: Well, yes, the pressures. I guess that's a good word. I think both coasts have differences, and you can characterize the people in the Midwest. Some of the characteristics that are lacking in the Midwest that you can find on either coast are quite important to this country. The Midwesterners really don't get themselves mixed up in a lot of things that the people on the coasts are exposed to and feel like they have to. I'm only speaking now just of the kind of solidness, the sort of integrity, the day-to-day approach to things. Of course, I'm trying to avoid the word "conservatism," but that's what I'm thinking all that way through this--that you find in sizable pockets in the Midwest.

Yes, I got along fine. I think they're some of the finest people I've ever known that reside in the Nebraska area. They're fine people.

Q: Would you talk about the educational problem, the VIP program, and that sort of thing. People are curious about that whole setup. You must have dealt with a lot of people.

Admiral Michaelis: Yes, we did. We had visitors coming out all the time.

Q: Is there a regular briefing session?

Admiral Michaelis: Yes, there is. I can't say how it is now, but at that time most of the visitors were to SAC, because, of course, there were two different reasons for going down to Omaha and Offutt Air Force Base. One was normally at the invitation of SAC, and that was marketing SAC. The other one was SIOP and a desire for information and that kind of inner sanctum that very few people have ever had a look at. So you went to Offutt with different reasons in mind. Very often, those two reasons would kind of get themselves mixed up, because the same man was the director of targeting as was CinCSAC. That's part and parcel to these sort of things.

It would have been a good idea, from my point of view, to have had JSTPS at Fort Ritchie, up here in the mountains of Maryland. That's a place where it's underground and reportedly the national command authority may or may not go there. There's a lot of places they can go. I think it would have been a little bit better to separate this joint staff from the very, very tight control they found themselves in. Of course, I'm a Navy guy, and that's what I would say, and I believe it.

Q: Can you say something about the security aspect of things out there?

Admiral Michaelis: I think it's very good. I think they were well equipped to give people a philosophic understanding of what the JSTPS did without getting into details. The details of the plan were, I think, carefully safeguarded. A lot of people thought they knew a lot about the plan when they knew there were X number of targets of a certain type or Y number of targets of another type. And that's what they could see at the secret level. They really don't know much about the plan, knowing that. They knew enough to sort of integrate it into their own thinking if they had a need to do so, but they didn't know much about the details. The details are just that--they were very, very detailed.

Q: What about the press and its relation to the base?

Admiral Michaelis: They saw a lot of the press at SAC, but we didn't see much of it at JSTPS. It was not encouraged. And, once again, we had press background briefings and so forth that we would provide if somebody wanted. But by the time the press had gotten pretty well briefed, things don't change real rapidly.

Q: So it was no longer hot news.

Admiral Michaelis: Yes, and the thing that changes out at JSTPS, of course, is the intelligence. The intelligence is the heart and soul of JSTPS. You do everything on the basis of how you interpret and evaluate and grade the intelligence.

Q: Can you say anything about the philosophy of targeting since it did burst into the press during the last year of the Carter administration when there was some shift in emphasis.[*]

Admiral Michaelis: The targeting plan is a product of the strategy of the U.S. That, of course, goes without saying, but I mean they almost slavishly followed it. The targeting guidance came right out of the strategy, and it was very carefully considered by the Joint Chiefs of Staff, by the Secretary of Defense, and by the President at a certain level of detail. That policy was very, very carefully followed. It was reviewed many, many times. Before we ever presented a new plan, a SIOP number this or a SIOP number that, we were always very careful to go back and see how well it conformed. If we found places where it could do a lot better job and it couldn't fit the policy, then part of our job was to go back and see if we couldn't get the policy changed.

Q: That was rather tough, wasn't it?

Admiral Michaelis: They were never the kind of changes that you're thinking about. The kind of changes that we ran into involved sometimes unnecessary inhibitions that you'd put on these at certain levels. No, it isn't too hard to get it changed. It took a while; it was a slow process. It was kind of like dealing with NATO: you're always 38 days from where you want to go.

Q: Then you were relatively happy at that assignment?

Admiral Michaelis: Not at all. Not at all.

Q: Oh, you weren't?

---

[*] Jimmy Carter was President of the United States from 1977 to 1981.

Admiral Michaelis: I was eager to get out of there. I learned a lot, and I look back on it, as you are able to do after a few years. You can look back on some period of your life when all those nifty things stand out rather than all the day-to-day soul-grinding things.

Q: After that tour of duty, you came to the one that you really thought was the greatest.

Q: Yes, I think it was as good as any tour I ever had. I was ComNavAirLant--Naval Air Force of the Atlantic Fleet.

Q: You were back in your original element then.

Admiral Michaelis: Yes. The reason that a type commander's job, I think, is a plum is that, one, there's always a lot to do. Two, you ought to be well equipped before you go there to do it. Three, you're usually there long enough to see some results on what you do.

Q: What was your period there?

Admiral Michaelis: Three years. For that type of job, that's what you're interested in to get that kind of tenure.

Q: Did you find things in relatively good condition when you went there?

Admiral Michaelis: Yes, based on the philosophy of my predecessor, who was an extremely capable man by the name of Bob Townsend.* Bob never should have left the Navy when he left that job. He should have gone on to get a four-star job, but he did leave the Navy. Yes, I found things in good shape. We were just getting into those terribly trying times where everything was used up in the Navy. We were getting around to the peak of

---

* Vice Admiral Robert L. Townsend, USN, served as Commander Naval Air Force Atlantic Fleet from 1 March 1969 to 29 February 1972.

requirements for the Vietnamese War before we ever got into the Christmas bombings and the Linebacker II.*

I found that to be the greatest challenge, of course, during that time and was constantly stretching those assets to cover two oceans. At one particular time, out of six carriers I had two of them in the Tonkin Gulf, two of them in the Mediterranean, and two back for getting ready to go. I didn't know whom to relieve.

We did some interesting things during that period. We had to get the USS Franklin D. Roosevelt out of the Mediterranean, because she had been there 10 months and was going to be there 12. She was going to be there over Christmas. You know, 12 months is too long without the families. The ASW carriers were just going out, so we took a CVS and rigged it up as sort of a poor man's attack carrier. We took off some of the ASW, we put some additional A-4s aboard, we gave them Sidewinders, and we called them strike fighters. Damn if we didn't send that little old ship over to the Mediterranean, just as big as could be, to relieve the Roosevelt and get it home.

Q: That must have been a revealing thing to the Soviets.

Admiral Michaelis: I don't know what kind of signal was sent to them. The revealing thing, I think, as much as anything else to them, was that we were short on what we needed to cover our commitments, but it also indicated a pretty strong determination to cover our commitments. Right at that time there was a great deal of concern in NATO about the constant loss of capability over there to feed the Vietnamese War. So we could not gap spots. I can recall some of them were kind of fun, and some of them were pretty dismal.

In conversations I used to have with Ralph Cousins, the VCNO at the time, and Bud Zumwalt, who was the CNO, I never could get them to make up their minds about doing

---

* In Operation Linebacker II, 19-30 December 1972, the United States resumed B-52 bombing strikes throughout North Vietnam. The Air Force bombers flew 729 sorties and helped persuade the North Vietnamese to return to peace negotiations.

these things.* I learned very quickly there that if you really knew something had to be done, and the political arm was not moving fast, you'd better get started with it. When we were in the 11th hour and they said to go ahead and do it, we were practically on our way. I don't know where I had gotten the money to take care of those things.

Q: That must have been transparent to them. They never came back and said why, did they?

Admiral Michaelis: No. Well, they would have found themselves standing a little naked in the middle of the street if they had asked why, because there was only one reason.

Q: I can see that is another reason why you made four stars too.

Admiral Michaelis: You know, in my particular case, it was right timing and so forth that came along. Then there was another one. These were the kinds of exciting things that you ran into as a type commander.

We got word on very, very short notice that we had to start getting A-4s into Israel during the Yom Kippur War in 1973. We had to get them in there. It's not very well known in many cases, but for a period of 48 hours we didn't have anyplace for air forces to land at land bases along the route going to Israel. So C-5s were about the only things that could get there.† By twisting the Portuguese arm hard enough, we kept the Azores.

Q: Yes, but we treated the Portuguese so badly.

Admiral Michaelis: Well, I don't know that we . . .

---

* Admiral Ralph W. Cousins, USN, served as Vice Chief of Naval Operations from 30 October 1970 to 1 September 1972. Admiral Elmo R. Zumwalt, Jr., USN, served as Chief of Naval Operations from 1 July 1970 to 29 June 1974.
† C-5s are large Air Force cargo planes.

Q: It's Tom Moorer's thesis that we had.*

Admiral Michaelis: There are a lot of things we could have done for them we haven't done, but this has been a great deal of national misconception. I can't much get into that.

The point I'm trying to make is we had to set up a plan to get A-4s into Israel with no bases. There was a 48-hour period when only the Navy could move things. Our plan was to hop airplanes all the way across--even fuel them en route from the fuelers that were coming up, or land them and send them on. Fortunately, we got the Azores back, and that first leg was done by sending groups of six and eight of these birds out with one KC-141, a big Air Force tanker. From that point on, it was a Navy show. We landed at the Azores and took off, landed aboard a carrier just inside the Mediterranean. Then we landed on another carrier over in the Mediterranean, and we flew into Lod with these birds delivered.† We delivered about 40 of these things that way. We did it in a very few days.

Q: And they were in operation the next day, weren't they?

Admiral Michaelis: They were in operation two hours after they arrived. Two hours.

Q: It was touch and go at that point.

Admiral Michaelis: Yes, it was. It was a very tight situation, and it was before the Israelis did the entrapment. The extraordinarily large flow of materials coming in at that time made it possible. But they were magnificent managers on the battlefield. An airplane would come in there and land, and two hours later it was loaded with weapons and ready to go. Two hours was not the turn-around for all of them.

Q: Your back was against the wall, I guess you'd say.

---

* Admiral Thomas H. Moorer, USN, served as Chairman of the Joint Chiefs of Staff from 3 July 1970 to 30 June 1974. His oral history is in the Naval Institute collection.
† Lod is a city in Israel; it is about 25 miles northwest of Jerusalem.

Admiral Michaelis: Yes. You do all sorts of things.

Q: That was an exciting operation.

Admiral Michaelis: It was exciting, and there were other exciting things that had to do with whether or not we should home-port carriers over in Greece.

Q: Wasn't that an idea of Zumwalt's?

Admiral Michaelis: Yes. It was a very difficult thing to translate to the sort of military-political mind all the things that associate themselves with the logistic requirements of putting a ship like that at anchor someplace without any real port facilities, without any industrial facilities, without even a dry dock in the Mediterranean the ship could go into if necessary.

Q: And on the other side of the coin, what were the advantages?

Admiral Michaelis: The advantages were somewhat ersatz, as far as I was concerned, and I made this as clear as I could to Bud. The idea, of course, was to get more use out of the same number of carriers. If you had a carrier home-ported in the Mediterranean, then you had to keep rotating only one carrier instead of two. From that point of view, that was a desirable thing to have happen, if you could keep up the readiness of the one that was there. The readiness was also peaked up before the carriers went to the Mediterranean, but they didn't have the target system there in the Mediterranean. They didn't have facilities to keep up ships the size of carriers, even in Toulon. So that became an almost constant exercise. Every week I was trying to tamp down something on this. Little by little, we got it across. Charlie Minter was up in OP-04 at the time.[*]

---

[*] Vice Admiral Charles S. Minter, Jr., USN, Deputy Chief of Naval Operations (Logistics). Admiral Minter's oral history is in the Naval Institute collection.

Q: Charlie went out there, and Stan Turner went with him.

Admiral Michaelis: We all went out from time to time. Charlie would call up and say, "I'm at the end of the tether again, Mike. You've got to come up. I'm out of control." So we worked as a team. I had no objection to home-porting overseas, but it had to be done in a reasonable way. The way that I call reasonable was going to cost a few more bucks than it was to do it the way CNO wanted it. The reasonableness equated to readiness. You can't put a carrier there and keep it ready. It's a very, very poor risk.

Q: Would it be any better with nuclear-powered carriers?

Admiral Michaelis: You always do better with nuclear-powered carriers, no matter what you're doing. You don't do any better just from the viewpoint of home-porting. Maybe I'm not understanding your question.

Q: I think in terms of readiness, for example.

Admiral Michaelis: In readiness, yes, of course. At the time when all of this was going on, the nuclear carriers were not going to be forward deployed, because they could move so fast with a train.

Q: It wasn't necessary to have them stationed.

Admiral Michaelis: They could move into position a lot faster. When we used to send conventional carriers out for some special job, we used to start the oil tankers moving three or four days earlier, because they were slower. Those were the kinds of things. It was an interesting period.

Q: One thing on the home-porting. That was the human element, the family element. That didn't work out as anticipated.

Admiral Michaelis: Not as anticipated. Bud had the idea that the families were going to be eager for the experience and the excitement of going over and living in a foreign country. That's not part of our culture anymore. It is still part of our culture for unattached people, but it's not the case across the board with married people who expect to stay in one home port for a while and live off the American economy rather than a foreign economy. The kinds of things that needed to go into the foreign economy to try to Americanize it were pretty extensive. If you take a look at the concerns in Europe today, you'll find people don't go more than two miles outside their whole tour of duty.

Q: That wouldn't pertain to you.

Admiral Michaelis: No.

Q: It wouldn't pertain to me either.

Admiral Michaelis: No, but it was not given enough consideration. It was just like Bud Zumwalt changing the uniform. They sort of made up their mind they were going to change the uniform before they ever went out with their surveys and polls.* I got along fine with Bud, simply because I never had to serve in town with him. I was always out of town, so I could always be in that fine position of calling him from the field and saying, "Hey, Bud, you've got to do something about those Z-grams. They're killing us. Why don't you take about 50 of them and consolidate them into one, and maybe some of the inconsistencies will

---

* Admiral Zumwalt did away with the traditional white hat and sailor uniform for pay grades E-1 to E-6 and outfitted enlisted personnel in those grades in uniforms similar to those worn by chief petty officers. The change did not last; the traditional uniforms were restored a few years later.

be removed."* So it's always nice to be in a position where you can sort of phone in and be the helper as to how to make things go a little better, rather than have to be the executor from the headquarters end.

But that was a good job. We did interesting things. We were so busy that time just went fast, and we had comfortable places to live. The people down in Norfolk were good. It was an exciting time in that complex down there, because you had everything Navy within a distance of about 30 miles from the center of Norfolk. You had so much Navy down there that you could organize and plan almost anything you wanted with great facility.

Q: Was it a time of reduced budgets?

Admiral Michaelis: It sure was.

Q: Was this a handicap to you?

Admiral Michaelis: Yes, very much so.

Q: How did you circumvent it?

Admiral Michaelis: We did all sorts of things that were short term. We didn't look to the long term. We had no choice. The whole Vietnamese War was a short-term thing. How did you circumvent it? We really didn't circumvent all of it. We tried to manage around a lot of it. You were constantly doing things to stretch. You were constantly distributing shortages, to be very frank. We distributed shortages to minimize our lack of readiness. But that was during a period when we had already decided that it was time to cut back--with some promise of getting new equipment if we turned in old, which, of course,

---

* *Z-grams were consecutively numbered policy directives from Chief of Naval Operations Zumwalt that attempted to deal with such issues as enlisted rights and privileges, equal opportunity, and Navy families. Junior personnel viewed them much more favorably than did their seniors. See U.S. Naval Institute Proceedings, May 1971, pages 291-298.

never happened. We tended to turn the old equipment over too fast. But it was just as well that we did, because there was no way we could get any money to operate it anyway--that being the mood of the Congress at the time.

Q: And what about personnel problems? This was the time minority issues were coming to the fore.

Admiral Michaelis: Terrible. It was a very difficult time. There was a great deal of confusion when you started mixing the problems of race with leadership. We came up with some answers that were not necessarily sound. We just plain had to get back to fundamentals before we got things straightened out. It took a long time.

Q: This custom of circumventing the chain of command--did that bother you very much there?

Admiral Michaelis: I didn't think there was a whale of a lot of circumventing in my world.

Q: Well, I was thinking of the minority reps, or what have you, on ships who would tell the men that they had direct access to the CNO and didn't have to go through the skipper.

Admiral Michaelis: I used to get called by those people in Washington on a lot of things that were written, but I never had a time when it wasn't backed up. My intention was to stay with the chain of command.

Q: I'm sure it was, but . . .

Admiral Michaelis: And occasionally you have to get rid of a CO that just doesn't understand that. When they start getting in trouble with the race managers, you have to back up the ones who do understand it. This business of racial brewing has been going on for a long time. Way back when I was CO of the Enterprise there were racial skirmishes.

The policy was that there was no discrimination aboard a ship. Even in those early days we used to have to stick it out, but we took a very firm foot and tried to keep things balanced on each side. But during the period of 1973 to 1975 it was pretty bad. You were spending too much time. What did they call the blacks that they assigned to each staff? I'm trying to remember. They were liaison of some sort.

Q: Because there was a top one in headquarters.

Admiral Michaelis: Yes. I always had good, carefully selected people in this job. And I tried not to keep them in there, because most of the ones who were really worthwhile didn't want to run it. They wanted to get out and fly their airplanes, or they wanted to get out and work their weapons or whatever it was. They wanted to learn and get the broadening it takes to get advanced in the Navy, not spend all their time trying to level out all these race problems that came along. I always felt very sorry for them; I mean, I had a great strong feeling for them, because we were asking them to do sort of an extraordinary type of thing. If you're running a pig farm right, you shouldn't run into as many troubles as we ran into. That's my theory. I'm being a little disjointed here. Let me just see if I can put it a little more succinctly.

We had an extra layer of effort that was deemed necessary, because we had sort of let our situation get out of control to begin with. The objective is that it's always good to keep things under control to start with. I say control, and I mean exercise a proper degree of human understanding and also exercising the necessary parts that go with being in the military, as opposed to being a member of the civilian society. Although we always get a normal cross section of society in the military, you cannot treat the military like you treat the cross section of society. That is my opinion. I've never seen anybody in the military who tried to run a totally democratic arrangement that was successful.

Q: And you imply it all got out of balance at that time?

Admiral Michaelis: It all gets out of balance. Then to grab ahold of these things and try to pull them back in is like anything else where--I consult with a few people right now who I think are the greatest industrial ones out there. I think they are just magnificent at recovering when they have problems, but they are lousy at preventing problems. They let things get out of control too often. They spend three times as long recovering as they would have if they had spent the proper amount of time in preventing it. That's the way it is in dealing with all human beings. I don't have all the answers. I have a few basic principles that I like to live with, and I'm old enough to be able to spout them.

Q: When you examine that whole situation, what would you say was at the root of it? The failure in great numbers of reenlistment and that sort of thing? Was this the thing that impelled this into being with Zumwalt?

Admiral Michaelis: I think that Zumwalt had really the best interests of the Navy at heart. I don't question his motives, which I've heard questioned many times. I believe that he moved too fast. Whenever he couldn't get people agreed in his line of thought, he set up special channels to handle it. Such a thing is an anathema to the military system. You can't live off of a kitchen cabinet, you know.[*] You've got to live off of your chain of command. If it's not good enough, then get it good enough and make it work. But you can't parallel everything. That was my view. He was eager. He had a lot of good ideas. He tried to rebuild Rome in 15 minutes.

Q: I heard him speak at the Army-Navy Club very early on in the days of the Z-grams. He was really alarmed at the rate of reenlistment that was way down. I always thought that was the motivating factor.

Admiral Michaelis: I think it was. I think Bud had made up his mind that he was going to try to liberalize the Navy to the degree that he could. But that liberalization got in the

---

[*] One of the criticisms of Admiral Zumwalt was that he restricted his dialogue to a small coterie advisers--a sort of "kitchen cabinet."

hands of promoters that just moved it way beyond the kind of bounds that you like to keep it in. It's nothing I wouldn't say to Bud if he were sitting right where you are. I think the combination that the country was going through was no help to whoever the CNO was going to be.

Q: No.

Admiral Michaelis: The combination of events: fighting a very unpopular war, fighting a go-nowhere war, seeing a lot of money and a lot of resources of the United States being used for things that were not really aimed at strong goals, which meant deprivation in some areas. Whether deprivation was there or not, it was certainly promoted during the period. I think we were caught right at a time when it was obvious that the ratio of losses and so forth in lesser minorities was out of proportion to their representation in the population.[*] That, plus a lot of other things, caused a peaking of the race problems that we had. Once they're encouraged and once the country is sort of encouraged to disobey, it creeps over into the military. The whole country found they didn't have to obey on anything.

Q: It's almost a state of revolt.

Admiral Michaelis: Sure. This is as close as I hope we'll ever get. The thing that bothered me more than anything else, when I think about this, was that any time there was a process or mechanism or apparatus that would help in the control of the problems you might have, it was dismantled as soon as it was found that it was standing in the way of anything that was called "rights." This is not a good subject for me to get on.

Q: It may not be a good subject, but it underscores so much of life.

Admiral Michaelis: Yes, it really does.

---

[*] Among ground troops in particular a higher number of blacks were killed in Vietnam than their proportion within the nation's overall population.

Q: Even today.

Admiral Michaelis: There are tremendous lessons to have been learned in the last 10 or 15 years that I'm not real sure are getting recorded. I think there are some people that caused this kind of trouble in the first place who are doing their very best to make sure that they're not recorded. So I've registered all my biases now.

Q: I think that's a good thing. They are recorded, literally recorded. You can think of nothing else in that three-year period that should get on the record here?

Admiral Michaelis: No, it was the most exciting day-to-day routine that you can have as a commander. I think the kinds of problems that are dealt with every day and the opportunities to do something about them are very good for a type commander.

My son used to say, "Dad, if I could have any job I wanted in the Navy, what would you recommend?"

And I'd say, "Whatever your warfare specialty is, be a type commander. You're not going to go out and win any battles, but you're sure going to determine whether or not they're going to be won."

Q: What about the advent of the big new carriers coming on the scene?

Admiral Michaelis: During that period we had under construction the Nimitz and the Eisenhower.[*]

Q: That's what I mean. You had those under construction. You had the USS Enterprise in being.

---

[*] The USS Nimitz (CVN-68) was commissioned 3 May 1975; the USS Dwight D. Eisenhower (CVN-69) was commissioned 18 October 1977.

Admiral Michaelis: We had an interesting thing happen in those days. As you recall, we had supposedly three carriers that Jimmy Holloway did a good job of promoting, the same kind of economy that is being stated this year for the carrier buy.[*] It turned out to be two rather than three; they dropped the third one and reinstated it later at a much higher cost.

One of the things that was very interesting that you learn as type commander was that you had better be well-informed for both the ships as well as the aircraft end of your carrier world. You need to know how the equipment that they're going to see in the future is going to affect the construction of the present. Carriers take so long to build and so long for people to decide they want them that these two ships, the Nimitz and the Eisenhower, came along without some of the equipment that they needed. It had to be put in them shortly after they went into service. The reason that they were not changed in midstream is that it would have opened the contract to an even greater degree than was opened by that shipbuilding plan that was going on.

Q: That will come in the next phase of your career. You didn't want to change the contract, but was it also because some of these features may not have been found tried and true when the ship was designed?

Admiral Michaelis: No, not really. The thing that came along with the new brace of airplanes didn't do anything to change it. The arresting gear was adequate, the catapults were adequate, but we had to have some tremendously big blast deflectors to take care of the F-14. That doesn't sound like much of a job, but it's a big job. It goes into the sort of magazine arrangement to handle the Phoenix missile which was part of the F-14, a very necessary part of our air defenses. We had to have a whole mezzanine built into the ships to take care of things that are called VAST, which is an automatic test system which, given the proper plug-ins, would handle all kinds of airplanes rather than just have this sophisticated test equipment for each type of airplane. So there were some big changes, and they were expensive changes that had to be made.

---

[*] Admiral James L. Holloway III, USN, served as Chief of Naval Operations from 29 June 1974 to 1 July 1978.

Nimitz went out on a cruise with none of the new aircraft aboard and came back and got its modifications. From that point in its life, it was a very, very modern aircraft carrier.

Q: But her initial cruise was . . .

Admiral Michaelis: Her initial cruise was with F-4s instead of F-14s.

Q: Is that unique in naval construction?

Admiral Michaelis: No, and it isn't a matter of construction. It's a matter of how you contract. Comparisons were made. Should we break the contract and get these things done now, the cost was going to be a lot more than to do them in a private yard than it would be in a naval shipyard later. It's very important not to break contracts when you know they're going to explode on you. Many, many times contractors are losing money, and all they're waiting for is the first excuse to break the contract. As soon as he does that, you find the product on the new contract costs you some fraction more than it did before.

Those are excellent carriers. Having only two reactors, they had all sorts of room for aviation fuel and conventional weapons. You should do anything you could do in a nuclear carrier to make your expendables more consistent with the fact that you have an almost unlimited supply of ship propulsion fuel. The nuclear carriers are magnificent. They have about 14 days of combat in them. Before you have emptied the aviation fuel tanks, you have fought at a high rate for 14 days. It's just unbelievable at the rate that you pump aviation fuel and use weapons in a high-sortie environment. So that meant you could send them anyplace, and they could fight for 14 days. In these slow-moving ships you wouldn't have to start out until later, and maybe you wouldn't have to send them at all. At least if they turned around and came home with the carrier softened up some political hard spot, why, and didn't fight . . .

Q: It certainly revolutionized strategy, didn't it?

Admiral Michaelis: It really did. In the very near future, we are going to be in a position to establish nuclear task groups. But unless you can do that, you don't get the full advantage that you would otherwise.

Why don't we go on to NavMat? I took office there in 1975.

Q: You might begin by giving me a thumbnail sketch of NavMat. The scope of it was tremendous.

Admiral Michaelis: It's like a lot of other corporate things. When you start to talk about the scope of NavMat, you include everything that's under it.

Q: It sounds like General Motors or something like that.

Admiral Michaelis: Yes, it does. It was 216,000 people or something like that. Let me tell you how that breaks down. There were five material commands, of which three were product associated, and two of them were services. There were the Naval Electronics Systems Command, Naval Air Systems Command, and the Naval Sea Systems Command. All those systems commands were product oriented, and the Supply Systems Command and the Facilities Engineering Command took care of just what they said.

Moving in below that, or sitting off to one side of that was the whole Navy system of the R&D centers or labs, whichever you prefer to call them. There were about seven or eight of those places, such as China Lake.

Q: And NOL.

Admiral Michaelis: Well, NOL was a little different facility. That was called a GOCO--government-owned contract operator. I'm talking here about the ones that were government owned and government operated. Those included Dahlgren and White Oak and Warminster and so forth. These were under NavMat with some sharing of responsibilities with the Assistant Secretary for RES--research engineering systems. There was that group. There were the R&D test stations like Patuxent River.

Q: It had a lot of satellites.

Admiral Michaelis: Yes, a couple of satellites. Point Mugu, of course, had a lot of satellites. Then there were the eight NARFs--naval air rework facilities. There were eight shipyards. There were three ordnance stations. I guess there were about three of them. But when you totalled all of that up, if you wanted to include everybody, that is the Naval Material Command. It is really, pure and simple, the shore establishment of the Navy.

As a consequence, it's a different breed of life, normally, than most naval officers enjoy through most of their careers. I never had more than an absolute minimum of civilians in any organization I served in. In NavMat, if you count all the blue-collar workers and so forth, about 1.7% of your force was made up of naval officers. Over 98% was civilian. So anybody that takes up with NavMat and isn't used to dealing with a certain sort of system, learns a lot about it pretty quickly.

Q: It must have been a rather daunting assignment.

Admiral Michaelis: In 38 years in the Navy, I had only one bad year. That was the first year in NavMat. I had good years in the second and third.

Q: I know you were reported to have said rather plaintively that you were spending 90% of your time on one element--the contract area.

Admiral Michaelis: That's right. That was terrible. I'll tell you one of the reasons it was bad that first year. I think I'm saying this in good faith. The Navy world was being ambivalent about the material job. They didn't know if they wanted a Chief of Naval

Material or not. They didn't know if they wanted something like OP-04 in OpNav.[*] They didn't know whether they wanted to do away with it and go back to some kind of a distributed bureau system. They really didn't know what they wanted.

Q: I thought they had taken the step forward when they set up the whole system.

Admiral Michaelis: They did. When you have a bureau system well entrenched, it's very hard to put a layer on top of it. It isn't impossible, and it's taking place, but it takes a long time. NavMat, I think, has had a less-then-resplendent history. I'm speaking now of NavMat as a corporate body sitting on top. How to define exactly how you want that corporate headquarters to work is a very difficult thing. I used to argue for a great deal more decentralization than we had--with some very good tight controls--but I didn't have the control of the dollars that I wanted, nor did I have control of the people that I needed in order to establish a decentralized system.

Q: Both of them essential.

Admiral Michaelis: I worked a lot on that when I was there, and I got in a lot of trouble. I got to the place where people were determined that I was not going to be successful. That happens all the time. But when it happens, it takes longer to get the job done, I think. Then, superimposed on this whole thing, was this nice shipyard claim thing that was handed to me the first day I walked into the job. That really was the most . . .

Q: A nest of vipers.

Admiral Michaelis: It's the most mentally destabilizing. You start off by saying, well, you'll get on top of this. And then you look at the history of the thing, and you realize it hadn't been solved in five years. It was doing nothing but getting worse. There were very, very

---

[*] OP-04--Deputy Chief of Naval Operations (Logistics).

strong powers and influences that would not permit it to get well until there was an extremely strong position taken by the Secretary of Defense and an agreement with Congress that something had to be done about it.

Q: And even then . . .

Admiral Michaelis: Even then it was traumatic. So no matter whether it was an imperfect solution or not, I'm glad there was a sense that prevailed and realized you're either going to settle, or you're in for another 20 years.

Now I'll address one of my great biases, and that is that the legal world has it within them to keep you in litigation for as many years as there are between the first and second coming of Christ. (I may change a few words when you give me the script back.) One of my biggest problems was with lawyers.

Q: That's their livelihood, of course.

Admiral Michaelis: Yes. Well, I think lawyers in the government sometimes lose their lawyer-client perspective. If I hire you as a lawyer, as a civilian, I want you to let me know what the law is, but I expect you to work about four times as hard figuring out how I can do what I want to do, rather than tell me all the reasons why I can't do it. That's enough said about lawyers, but that describes the general counsel of the Navy in that particular period. Fortunately, we got Graham Claytor aboard, who's a good lawyer and a good businessman.[*]

Let me get back to that first year, because it was sort of ambivalent. I wanted to make sure that whatever the CNO wanted, I was going to do it.[†] If he wanted me to

---

[*] W. Graham Claytor, Jr., served as Secretary of the Navy from 1977 to 1979.
[†] Admiral James L. Holloway III, USN, was then CNO.

dismantle it, then I'd dismantle it.* But I also gave him the choice that if he wanted to have a strong Naval Material Command, he was going to have to support it.

Q: It was directly under the CNO, not under the Secretary then?

Admiral Michaelis: Back in 1966 we went under the unilinear system in declaration, but our rudder was a little broken getting anybody aimed that way. We didn't quite get the ship's head changed as fast as it should. The time came when it was decided there would be a NavMat. I think a good deal of sense prevailed.

I got a three-star position to get the man I wanted. I picked the best businessman in uniform to come in and help me. He was a supply officer, Vince Lascara.† There is no question that he was the best naval officer businessman, probably in the history of the Navy. Anyway, I held out for this, and I got it.

Q: Had you known him before and his qualifications?

Admiral Michaelis: Oh, yes. He was my supply officer on the Enterprise.

Q: Oh, I see.

Admiral Michaelis: He had also survived an eight-year period with Rickover in which Rickover thought so much of him that he made Vince his public affairs officer, as well as trying to keep Rickover out of trouble in the contracting world. So he was a procurement expert and a man who knew how to be a naval officer at the same time. You can't get a better combination than that.

---

* In 1985, a few years after this interview, Secretary of the Navy John Lehman disestablished the Naval Material Command and redistributed functions among the various systems commands. For a summary of the reorganization, see Norman Polmar, "The U.S. Navy: Command Changes," U.S. Naval Institute Proceedings, December 1985, pages 156-157.
† Vice Admiral Vincent A. Lascara, SC, USN, became the Vice Chief of Naval Material.

Q: No. He was very fortunate in that he had that background with Rickover. I think that would be helpful to you too.

Admiral Michaelis: It made him hard and tough. He was a great help. Things really started working out. I made sure that we set the organization up so that he didn't have to spend all his time administering. We set up a thing that we called chief staff officer, a very, very bright captain brought in. We kept piling more and more and more details on him and gave him a little sub-staff to get things done. We would review these things with him maybe once a week. Vince was free for helping to get set up to solve these problems.

Q: You intimate that you had some real problems there which would cause some people to think you were not going to succeed in the job. What were these elements that you had to surmount in this first year?

Admiral Michaelis: Every year OMB would run another study on us.[*] They would make a recommendation, and sometimes it showed up in the halls of Congress as a recommendation that the Naval Material Command be disavowed, disbanded, or that it be cut to some arbitrary number of people. I'm speaking now of the headquarters. The real problem was that organizational changes were made without either enough people believing in them at the time or supplying the kind of discipline that would make it possible. It was policing the whole thing, making it work. OMB almost made a living out of NavMat, you know, and their investigating.

So we were constantly struggling with this thing. It's very difficult, when you're struggling, to keep an good open mind. What you'd like to do is to say, "Where there's smoke, there's fire. Some of the things they're saying must be very good, and I'll get them sorted out." But nobody had this much time, nor was the rationale for what they were stating that good very often. You didn't always get the best benefit out of those studies.

---

[*] OMB--Office of Management and Budget.

But a lot of it's straightened out now. Once those shipbuilding claims went away, at least from what I've been able to look at from out in the margin, things have gotten a lot better.

Q: I suppose it's like a festering sore that affects the whole body.

Admiral Michaelis: Not only that, you have a tendency to say, "I'm a terminal case. I'm just a cancer." You know, you can put it in remission and eventually get rid of it. You get that feeling it's going to be the death of you. So you must put all the time you possibly can, and you've got all these other problems piling up alongside of you that you have to tend to. So that all got pretty happy in the last couple of years. We learned how to cope with a lot of these things.

Q: Perhaps you'd better deal with that core problem at this point, then, in talking about the whole picture. You had a man in your employ who was helpful, I would think--Gordon Rule, was he not?

Admiral Michaelis: I never did figure out who he was helpful to, but he was very helpful. He was helpful to somebody, not very helpful to me.

Q: He was not helpful to you? He did work out some sort of a solution for one of the problems with the CGN-41 contract, which was a crucial one, I understand.*

Admiral Michaelis: You'll note that the solution he worked out didn't stick.

Q: No, it did not.

Admiral Michaelis: It had no way of sticking. And that's not what you think, because it became another one of the highly emotionally charged things. You could never tell when

---

* CGN-41 is the USS Arkansas, a nuclear-powered cruiser commissioned in 1980.

Gordon was taking an ego trip and when he really thought he was doing something that was essential. He made it sound like he was always doing something essential. But he was a very special guy. Do you know him?

Q: I've met him, yes.

Admiral Michaelis: You ought to get to know him, because he is a man who has, for good or bad, a hell of a lot of influence in the sort of year-by-year comings and goings of NavMat. And some of it's been very good influence, and some of it has just been the kind that you wake up in the middle of the night saying, "I hope nothing like this ever happens. I hope I never have to put up with anything like this." Some of it was that bad because he's a strong character and very, very ambitious, highly egotistical. Sometimes he plays things very well, and sometimes he plays them in a miserable way. So the solving of the CGN-41 was no solution at all, really. It was a solution, but it was one that could never stick. The courts would never let it stick. The Justice Department would never let it stick. Oddly, the Defense Department, outside of Bill Clements, would never let it stick.[*]

The good part of it, I think, was the fact that it exposed the ridiculi that we were dealing with every day in trying to continue to solve things with a non-solution approach. There was only one solution, and that was the one that was finally used. We had to go over and lick our wounds, and we had to pay the prices. We didn't know how to handle a lot of the blimpy things that came into those claims.

Once they're cleaned up, then you have enough that you can do some of the things that John Lehman is doing today. He is really doing the kinds of things, recognizing the necessity for, one, the contractors to make a profit; two, to align the budgets and real costs; three, a good sharing of the risks. Once you've established a good target cost, then the contractors should share the risk. If you put in a target, which we constantly did under Rickover, we would establish target costs for ships in which the ceiling was really the

---

[*] William P. Clements, Jr., Deputy Secretary of Defense, 1973-77.

target. Then we would put abnormally low share lines--95 to 5, some dumb thing like that--where it only cost the contractor 5% to overrun. That's no good; you're begging him.

Q: So was Rickover himself an impediment because of his philosophy?

Admiral Michaelis: Well, I think he . . .

Q: He wanted them owned by the government, didn't he?

Admiral Michaelis: Yes. That was what he came around to, and maybe that's where he was aiming all the time. I don't know. If that's where he was aiming, the route that he was taking to get there was quite dubious. And he didn't.

Q: He didn't, no.

Admiral Michaelis: He didn't. And there was a lot of damage done during that time. He enforced something that he had always--Rickover's always been a great one to lean on his AEC connection in terms of the regulatory system. He would lean on that to give him all kinds of authority outside of his immediate sphere that he could justify in terms of safety. For example, he didn't just select the reactor officers for the ships. He selected the engineering officers as well, because the leg bone hooks to the thigh bone and so forth. The reactor was hooked to the engineering department. When it came time for steam catapults to go off of reactors, you know, he came pretty close to getting that in his pocket too.

Q: So these were backstops.

Admiral Michaelis: Yes. And he had some good reasons for doing this; there's no question about that. But he was a better man at centralizing all of this, probably, than LeMay, and I thought LeMay was an expert. Rickover was better at it than LeMay. Of course, he had more authority behind him, because he was straddling both.

Q: Yes, he had the Hill behind him too.

Admiral Michaelis: Yes. If I was going to do NavMat all over again and I could do it without shipyard claims, I think probably I would do a lot of things that have happened since we've cleaned up the shipyard claims. So I think NavMat is doing pretty well.

Q: As one reviews the whole situation, it seems one of the core problems was the fact that the shipbuilders didn't think they made enough money on this, that they were losing money.

Admiral Michaelis: No, let me correct that. I'm going to be very, very strong about this. There were three basic things that were wrong. First of all, we started out with a total package requirement under McNamara. It was after McNamara had left; the hysteresis that goes into any big changes usually carries over a few years after the man who's injected it is gone.

Q: Naturally.

Admiral Michaelis: The hysteresis in this system said we got around to the real all-up McNamarian principle in such things as the 963, where we built 30 destroyers in a row.[*] We designed a shipyard to do it, and in the shipyard we built five LHAs.[†] We started out with nine; as the price kept escalating, we finally dropped back to five, and we recontracted. Now, in that full package we simply gave a concept to the competitors. We gave them a mission and said, "Now, tell us how to do this mission." We didn't design the ships as we usually do. We said, "Here's the mission." We oversaw what they were doing, so you were

---

[*] This was the Spruance (DD-963) class of destroyers, which the Navy obtained under McNamara's total package procurement concept from the Litton/Ingalls Corporation. For a detailed discussion of the program, see Michael C. Potter, Electronic Greyhounds (Annapolis: Naval Institute Press, 1995).
[†] These were the Tarawa (LHA-1)-class amphibious assault ships.

going to design them, you were going to build them, and you were going to do this whole thing under one fixed price.

Now, if you were going to do that, you'd better have a good crystal ball if it's gong to take you more than a couple years to do this. If you're just going to produce a widget, then produce it. If you're going to design a yo-yo and produce all that in one year, a fixed-price contract is good. What those contracts didn't have in them were escalation clauses. None. We were going along with a low rate of inflation at the time this was taking place. Sometimes if was 3%; sometimes if was 4%.

Q: Single figure contracted.

Admiral Michaelis: Yes, it had an incentive line in it. If you could build for less than your target, you could get a high percentage. If you ran beyond a certain--see, the way these things are set up is that if this is cost going out here, you're given a target and you're given a ceiling. Up above is the way--really, it should go the other way around. This is your margin of profit here. If you go to the ceiling, you lose all of your profit. So what you want to do is carefully select the target, a reasonable amount, and you hope that the contractor will beat the target in order to get himself some extra money. When he makes a buck, so does the government.

Q: And that's his incentive.

Admiral Michaelis: That's his incentive. That's why it's called fixed-price incentive. Well, under those conditions, without an escalation clause, you suddenly get into double-digit inflation. It was unbelievable what was happening.

Q: It just ruined the picture.

Admiral Michaelis: Just ruined them. The contractors were the second thing. You see, you could double your cost for inflation in a period of maybe only six years. These were long-term contracts. You were getting through these contracts for 30 destroyers, and besides that they overran the schedules badly because they were not prepared to build them. It was given to Litton, and Litton had never run a shipyard before. They were an aerospace company. They had a lot of good ideas on how to put the two together, but they didn't know enough about shipbuilding to really take on a big contract. Number two, they were long term. So you had plenty of time for these flawed contracts to work on you. Again I say, if it had been a couple of years, you'd have been all right. But if it's ten years, you're in deep soup if you don't have an escalation clause and you're subject to high or double-digit inflation. Point one.

Point two, each and every one miscalculated the problems of a rapid buildup to take on a big contract. McNamara's idea was to create some General Motors of the shipbuilding world and give them big contracts that they could bid on and give them to the country for a low price. They'd do all the work--both design them and build them. Now, when you do that, and you don't have a loaded-up shipbuilding facility, you have to go out and hire.

In every one of the three cases--Pascagoula, Newport News, and Electric Boat, they had to hire up at too steep a ramp.[*] So that last year's journeymen became this year's supervisors, whether they were ready for it or not. The overhead went to hell. Support services had to go a lot higher under those conditions, and that's havoc. It takes you years to recover from trying to build up too fast. There's one lesson that shipbuilders learn: don't try to go from this level up to this level if you're talking about time down here and you're short of time in this. If you try to get up here on this steep ramp, you're in trouble. And all three of them were in trouble. So what they were doing was badly overrunning. And when a contractor starts to lose and starts to lose badly, he starts finding out reasons why it's the government's fault. That's built in.

Q: He's in a state of panic almost.

---

[*] These shipyards were the claimants against the Navy under various contracts. Only Litton/Ingalls at Pascagoula, Mississippi, was involved in building the <u>Spruance</u>-class destroyers.

Admiral Michaelis: Well, he really is. And they found all sorts of things that they conjured up. The hard core in these claims might have been 11, 12, 13%. The rest of them, as Rickover used to call them, were fluff. They were very important fluff in some cases, but they were built up in cross-ship effects. In downstream delays they would state the government was late with a given piece of government-furnished equipment, which caused them to lose all of this time downstream because they had to wait for it to get in before they could do the other things. If you press a ship and get it out early, you take people off of this ship, and you begin to get cross-ship effects. They were able to manufacture--in some cases, with fair justification. But in many cases, not.

The third element, which was of lesser importance, came in the societal changes that were taking place. You know, how was your upward-mobility program? How was your affirmative action program? The contract negotiators for labor right at that time were getting things they never had in contracts before.

If you take those three things and put them in aggregate, you've got a very, very difficult time. It's something that you have the choice: you don't get the ships, don't buy the ships. Take the scrap level, transfer it to another yard, and do something. Whatever you're going to do, eat a big loss, get along without the ships until five years later when you can pick up what you can do. All of them are terrible alternatives so far as what your aim is in building ships for the Navy. Or do something about making an adjustment. Essentially, what they did when the time came was split the losses. By that time, they had ballooned to such a point. The first yard to recover, which has the best management of all, of course, is Newport News. They recovered magnificently. They were tough. They cut their overhead; they did all sorts of things.

Q: They had the benefit of more capital, didn't they?

Admiral Michaelis: They had the benefit of a conglomerate. All the shipyards are part of conglomerates now.

Q: That was coming into the picture, Secretary Clements and his insistence on the application of Public Law 85-804.

Admiral Michaelis: Yes, this was the Proxmire-Clements battle.*

Q: And in the shadows of Rickover apparently.

Admiral Michaelis: Oh, yes. He was violently opposed to what was being done. 85-804 simply said that in cases where it was to be the best national interest, you could recompense an organization or a contractor to the government beyond his contract with normal consideration. Probably the word "normal" was not in there, but it would give consideration--"consideration" being a legal term that says, "You've got to give me something in exchange for this." There has to be some benefit to the government--either forgive a debt or recompense you beyond the place that your contract calls for.

Q: There was a way out.

Admiral Michaelis: It was a way out. It's a statutorial way out. There was a Proxmire amendment made to this. The amendment said that if you declare 85-804 at any time and it costs the government more then $25 million, you must come before congress and report it. Congress will decide within 60 days whether they will hold hearings; if not, you're free and clear for money. There was a strong, strong determination by Rickover that those bloody thieves were not going to get away with this. His name kept being brought into it. It was just pathologically impossible for him to accept anything that would indicate even any kind of weakness in his system.

---

* William Proxmire, U.S. Senator from Wisconsin.

Clements got ahold of me one day and said we were going to go 85-804 and straighten these things up. Preparation time was very short, but there was some critical reason why he wanted to get going on this. I've forgotten what it was. Preparation time was very short. Considering that short time and the initial closure with the contractors, Rickover was saying, "If you go 85-804, you get these guys in and start negotiating with them, you are never going to get a legal determination on this. If you fail, it's going to make a legal determination even harder for the government." There was a lot of sense in what he was saying, but the flaw in his approach was, "Let's let the courts decide. That's what we've got the legal system for." Well, that all sounds good, but it's the worst thing that could possibly be done, in my view, for the question of getting on and building ships. Because when people are under litigation, they do not build good ships. They do nothing but put their very best people on litigation.

Q: The courts had been involved prior to this.

Admiral Michaelis: The courts had been involved several times.

Q: Newport News.

Admiral Michaelis: Yes. In all these cases, we're waiting for the ASPCA, which was the court of higher appeals set up under the government system. So he announced this; he put in some figures for each of the companies and said it will be in this neighborhood to settle with him on. They really collapsed his tent on the fact that he didn't have any real good bases for selecting those figures. As I think he recognized was going to happen, this was a shot in the dark for Bill Clements. He accomplished two things with this. First of all, he let the world know that he, Bill Clements, understood that these things ought to be settled, and they ought to get out of the way. I think there was some political hay for him. I think that in his heart of hearts he felt maybe he had a 30-70 chance of making it. There were some very, very strong forces opposing him.

Those were difficult days. We sat and negotiated with the contractors. They considered that with Bill Clements there, they had the upper hand.

Q: They were also very emotional, weren't they?

Admiral Michaelis: Oh, terribly emotional. Then when it failed, of course, Rickover said, "I told you so. Now you've made the litigation worse." It's hard to take something that's already worse and say whether it's going to get "worser" or not. So 85-804 was a very meaningful process.

Q: When you look at the situation and the settlement that came ultimately, wasn't it in that same direction?

Admiral Michaelis: It was 85-804. But all the way was paved with Congress. Rickover was put in his cage, and a strong Secretary of the Navy, who was also a lawyer, could smell a bad lawyer at 100 yards.

Q: This was Claytor?

Admiral Michaelis: This was Claytor. He brought in a lawyer as his assistant to do this. Hidalgo was his lawyer.* Claytor had great faith in him. Claytor was told by the Deputy Secretary of Defense . . .

Q: Who was that at that point?

Admiral Michaelis: At that time it was Duncan.† Duncan said, "You're going to solve this thing, and I'm going to stand right behind you." So everything was lined up. When the

---

* Edward Hidalgo served as Assistant Secretary of the Navy for Manpower, Reserve Affairs, and Logistics, 1977-79. He was later Secretary of the Navy.
† Charles W. Duncan, Jr., served as Deputy Secretary of Defense, 1977-79.

Carter administration came in, they were determined they were going to do this job. So everybody knew when they came in they were going to do it. So when they started working the congressional rounds, they started doing all the things they had to do in preparation. Then it took two years, and they got it done well, rather than doing an 85-804 and shotgunning the thing over to Congress in a couple of days or weeks or so.[*]

These are the kinds of things you have to do when you start playing around with those kinds of millions of dollars. The settlement came out to about one billion and a half. But that was only about 35% of what was claimed. It was a very, very vitriolic period. Cripes, I could go on telling you about details of this thing forever more. But it can be read at better places than in my comments.

Q: You were at the helm, though. As you related the role of Rickover, it seems to me that at times he must have been treading on your authority.

Admiral Michaelis: Oh, he bypassed me completely after a time. You either play ball with Rickover, or he doesn't consider you in the ballpark anymore. Jimmy Holloway used to call me up and say, "What do you think about this latest proposition of Rickover's?"

And I'd say, "I don't know what his latest proposition is." He just walked right on by me. So I'd walk him right back again as soon as he'd walk on by me. So to me, if you put your hand into that, you're asking for a hell of a lot more than you'd like to bite off. Just throw it back into my court. Sometimes he'd call Rickover and tell him he wasn't going to do a damn thing about it. People were always that way with Rickover. I don't really want to get into Rickover.

Q: No, I know. You've talked about him prior to this, anyway, about your training under him.

---

[*] The Navy reached settlements with General Dynamics/Electric Boat and Litton/Ingalls in June 1978.

Admiral Michaelis: Yes, and I so admired the things that he has done. It is very difficult for me to view in good balance the last ten years.

Q: Don't you think age is a factor?

Admiral Michaelis: Oh, absolutely, absolutely. But you take a Rickover or a de Gaulle or anybody like that, and you can't turn them off. You can say, "Tomorrow you're finished." It's not possible.
    Well, sir, that brings me to the end of the end.

Q: When was the date of retirement?

Admiral Michaelis: August of 1978.

Q: You were there for three years.

Admiral Michaelis: A little over three years. I came in April, and I left in August.

Q: There's a great deal more to the story--I mean, the other aspects of this Material Command which either I hope you write or you will have another brief session in which you can talk.

Admiral Michaelis: I'll be glad to do that, but I'd sort of like to look over what I've got here. There may be things I'm going to be reminded of. There are things I can talk to you about that might be important to somebody down the line. Most of the things that had to do with NavMat would take so long to get down, and I'm really not interested in putting volumes and volumes on this thing.

Q: No, I'm sure of that. But just the highlights.

Admiral Michaelis: I think it will be helpful, Jack, to go ahead and get this thing done and let me look at it. Maybe there will be some things that I will say. I probably ought to talk into your machine a little more here.*

Q: All right, good. Thank you very much. This has been fine.

---

* Regrettably, there were no further interviews.

Index To

Reminiscences of

Admiral Frederick Hayes Michaelis

U.S. Navy (Retired)

A-4 Skyhawk
　　The United States supplied A-4 aircraft to Israel on an emergency basis during the Yom Kippur War in 1973, 141-143

Aircraft carriers
　　In the early 1950s the Royal Navy produced several innovations to improve aircraft carrier operations, 65-66; introduction in the mid-1950s of the capability to carry nuclear weapons, 67-70; as Chief of Naval Operations in the early 1970s, Admiral Elmo Zumwalt was unsuccessful in getting aircraft carriers home-ported in Greece, 143-145; construction of new ships in the 1970s, 151-152

Air Development Squadron Three (VX-3)
　　Based at Atlantic City, New Jersey, in the late 1940s and early 1950s, it helped develop tactics for the transition from propeller planes to jet aircraft, 46-48; unsuccessful attempt in the early 1950s to find a method for attacking railroads in Korea, 48-49; testing of new equipment from various manufacturers, 49-50

Air Force, U.S.
　　Development and testing of nuclear weapons in New Mexico in the early 1950s, 51-52; the Air Force was surprised in the mid-1950s when the Navy opted to develop a solid-fuel ballistic missile, Polaris, rather than using Jupiter, 71-72; in the early 1970s a large proportion of the Strategic Air Command staff was double-hatted to the Joint Strategic Target Planning Staff, 133-134; accommodation of visits to Offutt Air Force Base in the early 1970s, 136-137

　　See also Army Air Forces, U.S.

Air Force Pacific Fleet
　　Type command involved in the mid-1950s introduction of aircraft carriers' capability to carry nuclear weapons, 67-70

Aleutian Islands
　　U.S. battleship planes had difficulties getting back aboard ship because of fog during operations around the Aleutians in mid-1942, 21-22

Arco, Idaho
　　Site of Navy nuclear power training in the 1950s and 1960s, 84-86

Arkansas, USS (CGN-41)
　　Nuclear-powered cruiser that was the subject of contractor claims in the mid-1970s, 160-161

Army, U.S.
　　Efforts in the mid-1960s to develop sensors for use in Vietnam, 110-112

Army Air Forces, U.S.
A P-38 Lightning crashed onto the deck of the carrier Randolph (CV-15) in the summer of 1945, 34-35

See also Air Force, U.S.

Atomic Energy Commission
Oversaw the development and testing of nuclear weapons in the early 1950s, 51-60; supplied shipboard representatives when aircraft carriers began carrying hydrogen bombs in the mid-1950s, 68-70

Azores
Served as an intermediate stopping place when the United States supplied A-4 aircraft to Israel on an emergency basis during the Yom Kippur War in 1973, 141-143

Beers, Ensign Charles J., USN (USNA, 1940)
Managed to escape injury when the Japanese attacked his ship, the battleship Pennsylvania (BB-38), in December 1941, 18

Berlin, Germany
Visited by Naval Academy midshipmen in the summer of 1937, 11-12

Bombing
In the early 1950s the Naval Air Special Weapons Facility was established at Kirtland Air Force Base, Albuquerque, New Mexico, to test nuclear weapons and their delivery systems, 51-60; introduction in the mid-1950s of aircraft carriers' capability to carry nuclear weapons, 67-70; the ships of Carrier Division Nine operated in the Tonkin Gulf and conducted bombing operations against North Vietnam in 1967-68, 119-124

Bureau of Ordnance
Development work on guided missiles in the late 1940s, 41-42

Burke, Admiral Arleigh A., USN (USNA, 1923)
Did a superb job while serving as chief of staff to Vice Admiral Marc Mitscher in 1945, 36; as Chief of Naval Operations in the late 1950s, chose Polaris at the expense of Regulus, 72; provided a rough estimate of the number of ballistic missile submarines to be built, 91

Caldwell, Captain Turner F., USN (USNA, 1935)
Did excellent work on writing the rules of engagement during the Cuban Missile Crisis in the autumn of 1962, 93-95

Carrier Air Group 11
Operated in 1954-55 from the aircraft carrier Kearsarge (CVA-33) with a heavier all-weather capability than previously, 60-62

Carrier Division Nine
>Small carriers that operated in the Tonkin Gulf and conducted bombing operations against North Vietnam in 1967-68, 119-124

Chester, USS (CA-27)
>Heavy cruiser that in 1941 was one of the first ships in the U.S. fleet to be equipped with search radar, 14

Claims by Defense Contractors
>The Naval Material Command faced multiple claims from defense contractors in the 1970s, 156-170

Classified Information
>Strict security rules were observed during the Cuban Missile Crisis in the autumn of 1962, 95-97

Claude V. Ricketts, USS (DDG-5)
>Was used in the mid-1960s to test the concept of multinational manning, 89-90

Clements, William P., Jr.
>As Deputy Secretary of Defense in the mid-1970s, had a substantial role in settling contract disputes between the Navy and defense suppliers, 161, 167-169

Commercial Ships
>In the early 1960s, OpNav studied the concept of putting Polaris missiles on board NATO commercial ships, 90

Computers
>Study in the mid-1960s of tactical applications, 112

Congress, U.S.
>Testimony in the 1960s on the controversial F-111 aircraft development program, 117-118; role in settling defense contractors' claims in the 1970s, 167-170

Connolly, Vice Admiral Thomas F., USN (USNA, 1933)
>Testified against the controversial TFX/F-111 multi-service aircraft development program in the early 1960s, 117-118; in the late 1960s directed Michaelis to upgrade the strength and readiness of the naval air reserve, 127

Cooke, Lieutenant Commander Lemuel D., USN (USNA, 1939)
>Died while flying in Air Development Squadron Three in May 1950, 50

Crommelin, Commander Charles L., USN (USNA, 1931)
>Collected talented aviators when he formed Air Group 12 during World War II, 25

Cuban Missile Crisis
Captain Turner Caldwell did excellent work on writing the rules of engagement during the crisis in the autumn of 1962, 93-97

Demobilization
The Navy lost many well-trained individuals when they left the service soon after the completion of World War II, 38-39

Draper, Dr. Stark
Talented professor who taught a number of Navy students at the Massachusetts Institute of Technology in the late 1940s, 43-45

Dutch Navy
OpNav conducted a study in the mid-1960s on whether the U.S. Navy should help the Dutch Navy in its desire to operate nuclear-powered submarines, 106-109, 113-114

Dwight D. Eisenhower, USS (CVN-69)
Required extensive changes after completion in the mid-1970s in order to accommodate the F-14 fighter, 151-152

Education
Michaelis attended postgraduate school in aeronautical engineering, 1946-49, 40-46

Edwards, Captain David S., Jr., USN (USNA, 1934)
Was court-martialed in the late 1950s for his actions while commanding the fleet oiler Tolovana (AO-64), 81-82

Engineering Plants
In the 1950s and 1960s, prospective commanding officers of the aircraft carrier Enterprise (CVAN-65) studied in the Navy's nuclear power program, 83-86; frequency of refueling the Enterprise, 86, 97, 104; characteristics of the Enterprise plant in the mid-1960s, 98

Enterprise, USS (CVAN-65)
Training of prospective commanding officers in the late 1950s and early 1960s, 78-79, 83-86; frequency of refueling, 86, 97, 104; characteristics of the engineering plant in the mid-1960s, 98; handling qualities, 98; direct communications from Vice Admiral Hyman Rickover, 98-99; made an around-the-world cruise with nuclear escorts in 1964, 98-102, 106; won the battle efficiency E in the mid-1950s, 103; the heavy influx of guests was sometimes uncomfortable during operations, 103-104; nuclear power conferred an advantage when the ship operated in the vicinity of a typhoon during the Vietnam War, 105

F-14 Tomcat
The aircraft carriers Nimitz (CVN-68) and Dwight D. Eisenhower (CVN-69) required extensive changes after completion in the mid-1970s in order to accommodate the F-14, 151-153

F-111
   Controversial multi-service aircraft development program in the early 1960s, 117-118

F2H Banshee
   The F2H-3 version of this McDonnell aircraft was used to improve the all-weather capability of Carrier Air Group 11 in the aircraft carrier <u>Kearsarge</u> (CVA-33) in the mid1950s, 60-62

Families of Servicemen
   Were not eager to embrace the idea of having a U.S aircraft carrier homeported in the Mediterranean in the 1970s, 145

Fighting Bombing Squadron Five (VBF-5)
   Went through a training period in 1945 for possible combat duty, then performed in air shows, 37-38

Fighting Squadron 12 (VF-12)
   Training in the United States in 1944-45, prior to deployment, 25-27; took part in bombing strikes against Japan, Iwo Jima, and Okinawa in early 1945, 27-28

Fire Control
   Fire-control radar installed in the battleship <u>Pennsylvania</u> (BB-38) in early 1942, 21

Flight Training
   U.S. program for fledgling aviators in 1942-43, 23-25; importance of adequate training before facing the Japanese, 34

Football
   Michaelis had problems over the years with a knee injured while playing football at the Naval Academy in the mid-1930s, 8

<u>**Franklin D. Roosevelt**</u>**, USS (CVA-42)**
   Made an exceptionally long deployment to the Sixth Fleet in the early 1970s, 140

Germany
   Visited by Naval Academy midshipmen in the summer of 1937, 11-12

Greece
   As Chief of Naval Operations in the early 1970s, Admiral Elmo Zumwalt was unsuccessful in getting aircraft carriers homeported in Greece, 143-145

Guided missiles
   Early U.S. missiles, in the late 1940s, were plagued by difficulties, 40-41; Dr. Stark Draper of MIT did useful development work in the late 1940s, 45; development in the 1960s of the NATO Sea Sparrow, 115-116

Gunnery--Naval
In 1941 the outgoing 14-inch projectiles fired by the battleship Pennsylvania (BB-38) could be tracked on the ship's radar, 16

Helicopters
Role of rescue helicopters in recovering U.S. pilots downed during the Vietnam War, 121-122; use of lightweight HueyCobra attack helicopters during the Vietnam War, 122-123

Holloway, Admiral James L. III, USN (USNA, 1943)
Commanded the aircraft carrier Enterprise (CVAN-65) in the mid-1960s, during the Vietnam War, 103, 105; as Chief of Naval Operations in the mid-1970s, promoted carrier acquisition, 152; reaction when defense contractors made large claims against the government, 170

Israel
Received A-4 aircraft on an emergency basis during the Yom Kippur War in 1973, 141-143

Iwo Jima
Carrier aircraft supported the U.S. invasion of this island in February 1945, 28, 31

Japan
Initial carrier strikes against the Japanese home islands in February 1945, 27-28

Japanese Navy
Attacked U.S. warships at Pearl Harbor in December 1941, 17-19; use of kamikazes in opposing the U.S. invasion of Okinawa in the spring of 1945, 32-33; quality of Japanese aircraft, 33-34

Jet Aircraft
In the late 1940s and early 1950s, Air Development Squadron Three helped develop tactics for the transition from propeller planes to jet aircraft, 46-48; the necessity to change carrier operations to accommodate jets, 66-67

Joint Chiefs of Staff
In the early 1970s provided guidance to the Joint Strategic Target Planning Staff on strategy for the targeting of nuclear weapons, 138

Joint Strategic Target Planning Staff
Had the function in the early 1970s of integrating plans for the possible use of nuclear weapons, 132-138

Jupiter Missile
The Air Force was surprised in the mid-1950s when the Navy opted to develop a solid-fuel ballistic missile, Polaris, rather than using Jupiter, 71-72

Kamikazes
    Japanese use of during the closing stages of war in 1945, 32-33; damaged the carrier <u>Randolph</u> (CV-15) at Ulithi in March 1945, 34

Kearsarge, USS (CVA-33)
    Operated in 1954-55 with an air group that had a heavier all-weather capability than previously, 60-62

Kirn, Captain Louis J., USN (USNA, 1932)
    Commanded the aircraft carrier <u>Randolph</u> (CVA-15) in 1957-58, 76

Kirtland Air Force Base, Albuquerque, New Mexico
    Site of development and testing of nuclear weapons in the early 1950s, 51-52

Klouck, Chief Radioman Charles A., USN
    As a crew member of the battleship <u>Pennsylvania</u> (BB-38) in mid-1941, he had a major role in the operation of the ship's radar equipment, 14

Korean War
    Air Development Squadron Three made an unsuccessful attempt in the early 1950s to find a method for attacking railroads in Korea, 48-49

Lascara, Vice Admiral Vincent A., SC, USN
    Did an outstanding job as Vice Chief of Naval Material in the mid-1970s, 158-159

Litton Industries
    Designed the <u>Spruance</u> (DD-963)-class destroyers in the 1960s under the total package procurement process, 163-164; contract difficulties because of inflation in the 1970s, 164-165

Martin, Vice Admiral Harold M., USN (USNA, 1919)
    As Commander Air Force Pacific Fleet in 1955, sent Michaelis to various aircraft carriers that were getting nuclear weapons, 67-69

Massachusetts Institute of Technology, Cambridge, Massachusetts
    Michaelis studied under Dr. Stark Draper at MIT in the late 1940s, 43-45

McCampbell, Commander David, USN (USNA, 1933)
    Was a flight training instructor in Florida in 1943, later shot down seven planes in the Marianas Turkey Shoot in 1944, 24-25

McDonald, Admiral David L., USN (USNA, 1928)
    As Chief of Naval Operations in 1964, did not support an around-the-world cruise made by a nuclear-powered task force, 102

McNamara, Robert S.
Instituted many procedural changes when he became Secretary of Defense in 1961, 87; involvement in decisions concerning the number of fleet ballistic missile submarines to be built, 91-92; problems from his total package procurement process lingered even after he left the Defense Department, 163-165

Medaris, Brigadier General John B., USA
As Chief of Army Ordnance in the mid-1950s, was surprised in the mid-1950s when the Navy opted to develop a solidfuel ballistic missile, Polaris, rather than using Jupiter, 71-72

Medical Problems
Michaelis had problems over the years with a knee injured while playing football at the Naval Academy in the mid-1930s, 8; Michaelis had difficulty with his eyes as a midshipman, but they recovered, 10-11; the skipper of the fleet oiler Tolovana (AO-64) was court-martialed in the late 1950s, though he had mental problems, 81-82

Mediterranean Sea
Shore patrol arrangements in the late 1950s for Sixth Fleet ships, 75; the Sixth Fleet operated there with few fixed support facilities in the late 1950s, 77-78

Michaelis, Admiral Frederick H., USN (Ret.) (USNA, 1940)
Boyhood in Kansas City, Missouri, in the 1920s and 1930s, 1, 3-4; parents of, 1-5; sister of, 1, 3, 17-18; ancestors of, 2-4; as a Naval Academy midshipman, 1936-40, 3-12; study at Kansas City Junior College in the mid-1930s, 5-6; service as a junior officer in the battleship Pennsylvania (BB-38), 1940-42, 12-22; wife of, 22, 37, 44; received flight training in 1942-43, 22-25; served in Fighting Squadron 12 in 1944-45, rising to command the squadron, 25-36; children of, 37, 80; commanded Bombing Fighting Squadron Five in 1945-46, 37-40; attended postgraduate school in aeronautical engineering, 1946-49, 40-46; served from 1949 to 1951 in Air Development Squadron Three, 46-50; established and commanded the Naval Air Special Weapons Facility at Kirtland Air Force Base, Albuquerque, New Mexico, 1951-54, 51-60; in 1954-55 served as Commander Air Group 11, based on board the aircraft carrier Kearsarge (CVA-33), 60-67; brief tour in 1955 as special weapons officer on the staff of Commander Air Force Pacific Fleet, 67-70; served in 1956-57 as special assistant to the Assistant Secretary of the Navy for Air, 70-74; served in 1957-58 as executive officer of the carrier Randolph (CVA-15), 74-78; had a brief course of instruction at the Naval War College, 1958-59, 78-80; commanded the fleet oiler Tolovana (AO-64) in 1959, 80-83; underwent nuclear power training in 1959-60, 83-86; served 1960-63 in OpNav's Navy Plans Section, Division of Strategic Plans, 87-97; commanded the aircraft carrier Enterprise (CVAN-65), 1963-65, 97-106; served 1965-67 as Director of Development Programs in OpNav, 106-118; served in 1967-68 as Commander Carrier Division Nine, 118-124; served in 1968-69 on the staff of the DCNO (Air), 124-132; served 1969-72 as Deputy Director of Joint Strategic Target Planning, Offutt Air Force Base, Nebraska. 132-139; served as Commander Naval Air Force, U.S. Atlantic Fleet, 1972-75, 139-154;

served as Chief of Naval Material from April 1975 to his retirement on 1 August 1978, 154-171

Mines
In early 1945 a downed U.S. aviator was lost near Japan because he ditched in a minefield, 29

Minter, Vice Admiral Charles S., Jr., USN (Ret.) (USNA, 1937)
Outstanding individual who had served in the aircraft carrier Randolph (CV-15) during World War II, 26; as DCNO (Logistics) had a challenge in studying Admiral Elmo Zumwalt's plan to homeport a U.S. carrier in the Mediterranean, 143-144

Mitscher, Vice Admiral Marc A., USN (USNA, 1910)
While serving as Commander Task Force 58 in 1945, had his flag briefly in the carrier Randolph (CV-15), 36

Moorer, Captain Thomas H., USN (USNA, 1933)
As executive assistant to the Assistant Secretary of the Navy for Air in the mid-1950s, arranged for Michaelis to join the staff, 70

Naval Academy, U.S., Annapolis, Maryland
Imposition of discipline on midshipmen in the mid-1930s, 6-7; football, 8; remoteness of superintendents from the midshipmen, 8-9; aviation orientation, 9; summer training cruises in the late 1930s, 11-12

Naval Air Special Weapons Facility, Kirtland Air Force Base, Albuquerque, New Mexico
Did developmental work on nuclear weapons in the early 1950s, 51-60

Naval Air Force Atlantic Fleet
Felt a strain in providing ships and aircraft to meet the operational demands of the early 1970s, 139-140, 146-147; supplied A-4 aircraft to Israel on an emergency basis during the Yom Kippur War in 1973, 141-143; construction of new aircraft carriers in the 1970s, 151-152

Naval Material Command
Components of in the mid-1970s, 154-156; faced multiple claims from defense contractors in the 1970s, 156-170; subject to studies by the Office of Management and Budget, 159; problems with the total package procurement concept lingered in the 1970s, 163-166

Naval Postgraduate School, Annapolis, Maryland
Michaelis attended postgraduate school in aeronautical engineering at Annapolis and MIT, 1946-49, 40-46

Naval Reserve, U.S.
Efforts in 1968-69 to build the strength and readiness of the naval air reserve, 125-132

Naval War College, Newport, Rhode Island
Provided a broadening experience for students who were there in the late 1950s, 79-80

Netherlands
OpNav conducted a study in the mid-1960s on whether the U.S. Navy should help the Dutch Navy in its desire to operate nuclear-powered submarines, 106-109, 113-114

Nimitz, USS (CVN-68)
Required extensive changes after completion in the mid-1970s in order to accommodate the F-14 fighter, 151-153

Nitze, Paul H.
As Secretary of the Navy in the mid-1960s, was involved in Dutch efforts to obtain nuclear-powered submarines, 106-109, 113-114

North Atlantic Treaty organization
Supported in the late 1950s by Sixth Fleet operations, 77-78; the concept of a NATO multinational nuclear force was developed in OpNav in the early 1960s, 88-90; in the early 1960s, OpNav studied the concept of putting Polaris missiles on board NATO commercial ships, 90; OpNav conducted a study in the mid-1960s on whether the U.S. Navy should help the Dutch Navy in its desire to operate nuclear-powered submarines, 106-109, 113-114; development in the 1960s of the NATO Sea Sparrow guided missile, 115-116; lost some aircraft support in the Sixth Fleet in the early 1960s because of the requirements of the Vietnam War, 140

North Vietnam
The ships of Carrier Division Nine operated in the Tonkin Gulf and conducted bombing operations against North Vietnam in 1967-68, 119-124

Norton, Garrison R.
Whiled serving from 1956 to 1959 as Assistant Secretary of the Navy for Air, had a hand in getting the Navy into the Polaris program, 70-72; had a background in aviation, 73-74

Nuclear Power
Training program under Vice Admiral Hyman G. Rickover in 1959-60, 83-86; frequency of refueling the aircraft carrier Enterprise (CVAN-65), 86, 97, 104; characteristics of the Enterprise plant in the mid-1960s, 98; three nuclear-powered warships made a cruise around the world in 1964, 98-102; nuclear power conferred an advantage when the Enterprise operated in the vicinity of a typhoon during the Vietnam War, 105; OpNav conducted a study in the mid-1960s on whether the U.S.

Navy should help the Dutch Navy in its desire to operate nuclear-powered submarines, 106-109, 113-114

Nuclear Weapons
In the early 1950s the Naval Air Special Weapons Facility was established at Kirtland Air Force Base, Albuquerque, New Mexico, to test nuclear weapons and their delivery systems, 51-60; introduction in the mid-1950s of aircraft carriers' capability to carry nuclear weapons, 67-70; the concept of a NATO multinational nuclear force was developed in OpNav in the early 1960s, 88-90; in the early 1960s, OpNav studied the concept of putting Polaris missiles on board NATO commercial ships, 90; in the early 1970s, the Joint Strategic Target Planning Staff had the function of integrating U.S. plans for the possible use of nuclear weapons, 132-138

OP-05
Efforts in 1968-69 to build the strength and readiness of the Naval Air Reserve, 125-132

OS2U Kingfisher
Battleship planes had difficulties getting back aboard ship because of fog during operations around the Aleutian Islands in mid-1942, 21-22; involved in rescue of downed aviators in the Inland Sea of Japan in 1945, 30

Office of Management and Budget
Conducted many studies on the Naval Material Command in the mid-1970s, 159-140

Offutt Air Force Base, Nebraska
See Strategic Air Command

Okinawa
Carrier aircraft supported the U.S. invasion of this island in February 1945, 31-33; Japanese use of kamikazes, 32-33

Oriskany, USS (CVA-34)
Served as flagship of Carrier Division Nine during strike operations against North Vietnam in 1967-68, 119-124

P-38 Lightning
Army Air Forces plane that crashed onto the deck of the carrier Randolph (CV-15) in the summer of 1945, 34-35

Pearl Harbor, Hawaii
The ships of the U.S. Fleet were essentially based at Pearl in 1940-41, 17; Japanese attack on the fleet in December 1941, 17-19

Pennsylvania, USS (BB-38)
First became equipped with radar in the summer of 1941, 13-16; the outgoing projectiles fired by the 14-inch guns could be tracked on the ship's radar, 16; the ship

was essentially based at Pearl Harbor in 1940-41, 17; damage suffered during the Japanese attack on Pearl Harbor in December 1941, 19; steamed to San Francisco in late December for repairs, 19-20; fire-control radar installed in early 1942, 21; the ship was part of diversionary force during the Battle of Midway in June 1942, 21-22

Planning
The concept of a NATO multinational nuclear force was developed in OpNav in the early 1960s, 88-90; in the early 1960s, OpNav studied the concept of putting Polaris missiles on board NATO commercial ships, 90; in the early 1970s, the Joint Strategic Target Planning Staff had the function of integrating U.S. plans for the possible use of nuclear weapons, 132-138

Polaris Program
The Air Force was surprised in the mid-1950s when the Navy opted to develop a solid-fuel ballistic missile, Polaris, rather than using Jupiter, 71-72; Polaris was at the expense of the Regulus cruise missile, 72; in the early 1960s, OpNav studied the concept of putting Polaris missiles on board NATO commercial ships, 90

Polaris Submarines
In the early 1960s, OpNav conducted a study on how many fleet ballistic missile submarines to build, 90-91

Proxmire, William
U.S. Senator who had a hand in settling defense contractor claims in the 1970s, 167

Public Relations
The aircraft carrier Enterprise (CVAN-65) hosted a great many visitors during her around-the-world cruise in 1964, 98-100, 102, 106; hosting guests sometimes made operations uncomfortable for the crew of the Enterprise in the mid-1960s, 103-104; tours for visitors to the Strategic Air Command in the early 1970s, 136-137

Racial Unrest
Experienced in the Navy in the 1960s and 1970s, 147-150

Radar
Was little known in the fleet when it was installed in the battleship Pennsylvania (BB-38) in mid-1941, 13-16; fire-control radar installed in the Pennsylvania in early 1942, 21

Radford, Rear Admiral Arthur W., USN (USNA, 1916)
While commanding Task Group 58.1 in early 1945, summoned Michaelis to his flagship to talk about rescue of downed aviators, 29, 31

Railroads
Air Development Squadron Three made an unsuccessful attempt in the early 1950s to find a method for attacking railroads in Korea, 48-49

Randolph, USS (CV-15/CVA-15)
   Aircraft carrier that went into service in 1944, 25-27; took part in bombing strikes against Japan, and Iwo Jima, and Okinawa in early 1945, 27-30; damaged by a kamikaze hit while at Ulithi Atoll in March 1945, 34; was hit by an Army Air Forces P-38 in the summer of 1945, 34-35; modernized with a new bow and angled deck in the mid-1950s, she was a crowded ship, 74-75; deployments to the Mediterranean in the late 1950s, 75-76

Refueling at Sea
   The aircraft carrier Enterprise (CVAN-65) kept tanker aircraft in alert status on the flight deck during her around-the-world cruise in 1964, 100

Rescue at Sea
   The rescue of downed U.S. aviators off Japan in 1945 was frequently difficult, 29-31

Rescue on Land
   Role of rescue helicopters in recovering U.S. pilots downed during the Vietnam War, 121-122

Research and Development
   In the early 1950s the Naval Air Special Weapons Facility was established at Kirtland Air Force Base, Albuquerque, New Mexico, to test nuclear weapons and their delivery systems, 51-60; the Air Force was surprised in the mid-1950s when the Navy opted to develop a solid-fuel ballistic missile, Polaris, rather than using Jupiter, 71-72; efforts in the mid-1960s to develop sensors for use in Vietnam, 110-112; study in the mid-1960s of tactical applications of computers, 112; Navy organizational structure for R&D in the 1960s, 112-113; development in the 1960s of the NATO Sea Sparrow guided missile, 115-116

Ricketts, Admiral Claude V., USN (USNA, 1929)
   As Vice Chief of Naval Operations in the early 1960s, was interested in plans for a NATO multinational nuclear force, 88-90; supported an around-the-world cruise by a nuclear-powered task force until his death in 1964, 102

Rickover, Vice Admiral Hyman G., USN (USNA, 1922)
   Ran the Navy's nuclear power training program in 1959-60, 84-86; was a difficult, impatient man to be around, 85-86; habit of communicating directly with the reactor officer of the aircraft carrier Enterprise (CVAN-65) in the mid-1960s, 98-99; would have preferred if the 1964 around-the-world cruise of a nuclear-powered task force could have been made with no stops at all, 104-105; used the services of an outstanding Supply Corps officer, Vincent Lascara, 158-159; took a strident position with regard to shipbuilders' claims in the 1970s, 161-163, 166-170; age was a problem during his final years on active duty, 170-171

Royal Navy
   Produced several innovations in the early 1950s to improve aircraft carrier operations, 65-66

Rule, Gordon
   Civilian executive who worked with the Naval Material Command on shipbuilding claims in the 1970s, 160-161

Rules of Engagement
   Captain Turner Caldwell did excellent work on writing the rules during the Cuban Missile Crisis in the autumn of 1962, 93-97

Sea Sparrow Missile
   Development in the 1960s of the NATO Sea Sparrow surface-to-air missile, 115-116

Seventh Fleet, U.S.
   The ships of Carrier Division Nine operated in the Tonkin Gulf and conducted bombing operations against North Vietnam in 1967-68, 119-124

Shore Patrol
   Arrangements in the Mediterranean and Western Pacific in the late 1950s, 75

Single Integrated Operational Plan
   In the early 1970s, the Joint Strategic Target Planning Staff had the function of integrating U.S. plans for the possible use of nuclear weapons, 132-138

SIOP
   See Single Integrated Operational Plan

Sixth Fleet, U.S.
   Shore patrol arrangements in the late 1950s, 75; NATO commitments, 77; operated with few fixed support facilities in the late 1950s, 77-78; had an ASW carrier in an attack role in the early 1970s in order to get the Franklin D. Roosevelt (CVA-42) home from a long deployment, 140; as Chief of Naval Operations in the early 1970s, Admiral Elmo Zumwalt was unsuccessful in getting aircraft carriers home-ported in Greece, 143-145

Smith, Captain Daniel F., Jr., USN (USNA, 1932)
   Commanded the carrier Randolph (CVA-15) in 1956-57, 76

Smith, James Hopkins
   Served 1953-56 as Assistant Secretary of the Navy for Air, 70

Spruance (DD-963)-Class Destroyers
   Designed in the 1960s under the total package procurement process, 163-164; contract difficulties because of inflation in the 1970s, 164-165

Strategic Air Command, U.S.
   In the early 1970s a large proportion of the Strategic Air Command staff was double-hatted to the Joint Strategic Target Planning Staff, 133-134

Strategy
Work of the Strategic Plans Division of OpNav in the early 1960s, 88; in the early 1970s, the Joint Strategic Target Planning Staff had the function of integrating U.S. plans for the possible use of nuclear weapons, 132-138

Strean, Rear Admiral Bernard M., USN (USNA, 1933)
Commanded the carrier Randolph (CVA-15) in 1958-59, 76; commanded a nuclear-powered task force that went around the world in 1964, 101-102

Submarines
In the early 1960s, OpNav conducted a study on how many fleet ballistic missile submarines to build, 90-91; OpNav conducted a study in the mid-1960s on whether the U.S. Navy should help the Dutch Navy in its desire to operate nuclear-powered submarines, 106-109, 113-114

Sweden
Development efforts in the 1960s on submarine fuel cells and fighter attack aircraft, 114-115

Systems Analysis
Introduced to Department of Defense decision-making in the early 1960s, 87, 92-93

TFX
See F-111

Tactics
Based at Atlantic City, New Jersey, in the late 1940s and early 1950s, Air Development Squadron Three helped develop tactics for the transition from propeller planes to jet aircraft, 46-48; development in the 1950s of the loft method for delivering nuclear bombs, 54, 56-57; study in the mid-1960s of tactical applications of computers, 112

Total Package Procurement
Problems from this Robert McNamara process lingered into the 1970s, after he had left the Defense Department, 163-166

Tolovana, USS (AO-64)
Skipper in the late 1950s was court-martialed, although he had mental problems, 81-82; didn't have enough well-trained crew members in 1959, 82-83; was a challenging command for Michaelis, 82-83

Training
Summer cruises by Naval Academy midshipmen in the late 1930s, 11-12; flight training program for fledgling aviators in 1942-43, 23-25; Fighting Squadron 12 trained in the United States in 1944-45, prior to deployment, 25-27; importance of adequate training of U.S. pilots before facing the Japanese, 34; amount of training

needed to operate successfully with various types of Navy equipment, 62-64; instruction in nuclear power, 1959-60, 83-86

Ulithi Atoll

A Japanese kamikaze plane damaged the carrier Randolph (CV-15) at Ulithi in March 1945, 34

VBF-5

See Fighting Bombing Squadron Five (VBF-5)

VF-12

See Fighting Squadron 12 (VF-12)

VX-3

See Air Development Squadron Three (VX-3)

Vietnam War

Nuclear power conferred an advantage when the aircraft carrier Enterprise (CVAN-65) operated in the vicinity of a typhoon during the war, 105; efforts in the mid-1960s to develop sensors for use in Vietnam, 110-112; the ships of Carrier Division Nine operated in the Tonkin Gulf and conducted bombing operations against North Vietnam in 1967-68, 119-124; role of rescue helicopters in recovering U.S. pilots downed during the bombing of North Vietnam, 121-122; use of lightweight HueyCobra attack helicopters during the Vietnam War, 122-123; enemy submarines did not pose a threat to U.S. carriers operating on Yankee Station, 123-124; in the late 1960s the war drained resources from other areas, 132; put heavy demand on naval aviation in the early 1970s, 139-140, 146-147

Walker, Lieutenant Commander Thomas J. III, USN (USNA, 1939)

Was involved in the early 1950s in the development and testing of nuclear weapons to be used by Navy aircraft, 51

Walleye

Smart, TV-guided bomb used against North Vietnam in the late 1960s, 119-120

Weather

Battleship planes had difficulties getting back aboard ship because of fog during operations around the Aleutian Islands in mid-1942, 21-22; Carrier Air Group 11 operated in 1954-55 from the aircraft carrier Kearsarge (CVA-33) with a heavier all-weather capability than previously, 60-62; conditions when a nuclear-powered task force made an around-the-world cruise in 1964, 101; nuclear power conferred an advantage when the aircraft carrier Enterprise (CVAN-65) operated in the vicinity of a typhoon during the Vietnam War, 105

Yom Kippur War

The United States supplied A-4 aircraft to Israel on an emergency basis during this war in the autumn of 1973, 141-143

Zumwalt, Admiral Elmo R., Jr., USN (USNA, 1943)
As Chief of Naval Operations in the early 1970s, had difficulty finding resources to match commitments, 140-141; as CNO was unsuccessful in getting aircraft carriers homeported in Greece, 143-145; was challenged on some of his mandates concerning personnel during his tenure as CNO, 145-150